For Such a Time as This

For Such a Time as This
Evanston Killings, Election, Ethics Consult

KENNETH L. VAUX

WIPF & STOCK · Eugene, Oregon

FOR SUCH A TIME AS THIS
Evanston Killings, Election, Ethics Consult

Copyright © 2013 Kenneth L. Vaux. All rights reserved. Except for brief quotations in critical publications or reviews, no part of this book may be reproduced in any manner without prior written permission from the publisher. Write: Permissions, Wipf and Stock Publishers, 199 W. 8th Ave., Suite 3, Eugene, OR 97401.

New Revised Standard Version Bible. Copyright © 1989, Division of Christian Education of the National Council of the Churches of Christ in the United States of America. Used by permission. All rights reserved.

New International Version®, NIV®. Copyright © 1973, 1978, 1984 by Biblica, Inc.™ Used by permission of Zondervan. All rights reserved worldwide.

New American Standard Bible®, NASB®. Copyright © 1960, 1962, 1963, 1968, 1971, 1972, 1973, 1975, 1977, 1995 by The Lockman Foundation. Used by permission. All rights reserved.NAB

Wipf & Stock
An Imprint of Wipf and Stock Publishers
199 W. 8th Ave., Suite 3
Eugene, OR 97401

www.wipfandstock.com

ISBN 13: 978-1-55635-942-2

Manufactured in the U.S.A.

To Sara, my partner in life's journey,
the children and grandchildren, the students, fellow parishoners,
and colleagues—all who have been what it is all about.

Contents

Acknowledgments ix

Part One

- One   Election, 2012   3
- Two   Excursus: George McGovern   9
- Three   Booklet on 2012 Election and Excursus: Theology of the Presidential Candidates   14
- Four   Itinerary in Ohio: October 2012   33
- Five   Homily: Come Labor On   44
- Six   Superstorm Sandy   49
- Seven   Sunday in the Park, or a First Corinthians Study   52

Part Two

- Eight   Election Countdown   97
- Nine   Obama and Romney Election Night Speeches   100
- Ten   Rachel Maddow's Election Litany   102
- Eleven   Booklet on 2008 Election   106
- Twelve   Essay on Interfaith Hermeneutics   121

Thirteen	Aftermath of the Election: War, Sexuality, Interfaith Events	142
Fourteen	Advent Scriptural Reflections	151
Fifteen	More Shootings in Evanston, Illinois	156
Sixteen	Obama in Newtown	159
Seventeen	Homily, Second Presbyterian Church—Getting Bolder, Bigger, and Better	165
Eighteen	Excursus: Last Days of 2012	173

Acknowledgments

I WISH TO THANK Christian Amondson at Wipf and Stock Publishers for his leadership on this project, among many others at Wipf and Stock. I must thank Diane Capitani for her invaluable editorial guidance during the creation of this manuscript. Thanks also to Mike van Mantgem for his copyediting acumen to help this work find its final form.

Part One

One

Election, 2012

Sermon delivered to United Pastors in Mission, Cleveland, Ohio; Chapel, Muskingum College, New Concord, Ohio; and Mt. Moriah AME Church, Cleveland, Ohio (October).

My "bona fides" seem dubious in this heated-up election season. Fifty years ago I was the State of Ohio Orator, delivering an oration in a national competition entitled "Modern Science: Man's Salvation or Doom." Despite the first place vote of the President of the American Speech Association, I lost. (So did my role model, George McGovern—a true orator—philosopher, and later, presidential candidate.) "Too theological and triumphalist," cited my judges' evaluations. Yet, still, here I am, holding forth with those same religious pretensions/suppositions. I'll also ride on the coattails of our Muskie Football All American—Bill "Cannonball" Cooper, who was the star pitcher on the baseball team of which I played first base and wielded an "A-Rod"-like bat—(few hits)—even though I wore the number 4 and was called "Babe," at Bill's insistence. And again, here, fifty years later, I still wield the same quivering club. Just call me Pablo Sandoval. Any doubts about my (big man on campus) delusions?

One week ago, as I write this, I arrived in my old Ohio stomping ground with grand illusions of delivering this key "swing state" for the Obama column. I had been delayed in my departure from Chicago by a killing just near our Evanston home. Dajae Coleman, an exemplary fourteen-year-old—good scholar, promising basketball player, church leader; just a "good all-round kid"—had been accidentally shot in the chest by a wild flurry of shots from an automatic pistol. My neighbor,

Wes Woodson (he lives at 1702, we at 1615 Ashland) had reportedly received a rumor that someone had stabbed his cousin three hundred yards down Church Street at Evanston Township High School—the town high school. He rushed into the street and shot at the first group of students that he saw. Dajae fell and in a short time was dead. When I got there the next morning, the blood of Abel still cried from the ground. In a few days, I rode my bike down Ashland Avenue to see if my neighbor Wes Woodson was there. His son, Wes, had fired the shots. He had just been arraigned, bail had been refused, and a long imprisonment awaited. Wes Sr. was in the car, heaving with sobs. I shared my concern and support. I stopped to see him again after Dajae's funeral, sharing with him that some of the speakers had shared our view that two sons were lost on that fateful Saturday night.

The funeral was one of the most memorable of my life. It was at the African-American First Church of God—the same congregation that sponsored a community celebration for another beloved young athlete lost about fifteen years ago under similar circumstances. In our own gracious sanctuary of the First Presbyterian Church, the mourning crowd was aroused at the processional: "Jesus Christ is risen today!" Now some hundreds of freshman classmates, who had paraded down Dodge Street from Evanston Township High School in white shirts and dark pants or skirts, filed by the open casket. Many openly wailed, especially whites. Black brothers and sisters were stoically still and firmly resolved. They knew the trials of structural injustice and daily/nightly humiliations and hard knocks. They also knew and observed Dr. King's resurrection resilience. I again spoke with Wes Sr. on Sunday. As I cycled home, from across the street I heard a presence. It was Dajae, "Ken, I'm okay—go to Ohio." All who know me know that I'm not given to such esoterica. Still, I've long learned to follow such intimations. And here I am.

The present election has placed Ohio in a crucial role. We cannot therefore tolerate gubernatorial, state's attorney, super-donor, and Tea Party efforts to repress the vote with various disenfranchising measures like billboards that eerily warn, "We're watching you—you can be jailed or fined for 'fraudulent voting.'" The other side has also tried to revive Jim Crow laws, gerrymander districts, tolerate poor schools, incarcerate, redistribute wealth from the poor and middle classes upward to the very rich, and other forms of harassment of blacks, Hispanics, the poor, even youth. On the black scene, the proportion of persons removed from public participation today is exactly the same as it was during the era of slavery, predating Lincoln's Emancipation Proclamation. (See James Cone's *The Cross and the Lynching Tree* or Steven Spielberg's film, *Lincoln*.) This history of denial of liberty is a national shame and disgrace. Still, in the strange ethics of this nation, the "Great Passage" is seen as a tragic accident of history and not a deliberate, popular, and political act of injustice.

Disdain for poor and racial minorities, the ignoring of LGBT's (lesbian, gay, bisexual, and transgender) rights, paternalistic attitudes toward women and their proper authority over their own bodies, the willingness to compromise preschool care for children and Medicare/Social Security for the old—these are among the ethical issues embedded in the present election process. Fifty years ago, I found myself in jail in Hattiesburg, Mississippi, for aiding poor folk in the ministry regions of the Delta to register and to vote. Blacks had to pass a sophisticated civics test while ignorant whites were ushered through. Again, the old racist "dog whistle." Now, here I was again: the air of fear and intimidation was the same now in Milwaukee, Wisconsin, and Massillon, Ohio, as it was then in Meridian, Mississippi.

I've been a voter for fifty-two years—thirteen straight presidential elections. Theology has always determined my vote. When I was a twenty-one-year-old at Princeton, I followed the WASP crowd, voting for the upright Nixon over the suspicious, Catholic Kennedy. When rumor had it that JFK in the first debate had exchanged the good make-up for bad, forcing Nixon to sweat it out under the hot lights, I coined a new nickname—Tricky Jack and Hyannis-Gate—and thought myself a budding pundit humorist.

But in all these years I can't remember an election like this current one.

Regarding today's atmosphere of unprecedented torrent of cryptic mendacity, Garry Wills comments in his wry Will Rogers humor:

> Here is the Romney strategy: since you don't like what you've got, vote for what you haven't got. Whatever it is you haven't got, it is better than what you've got. That was supposed to be enough to secure election after what we've got—Obama's apparent economic failure. But the Romney campaign is taking what-you-haven't-got-ism to new heights of what–you-mustn't-know-ism. It supposes that revealing any details of what you haven't got will just distract from the fact that you haven't got it. Vote for whatever instead. (*New York Review of Books*, Nov. 8, 2012, 63)

Leaving everyone in the dark is not the only "Romnesia" of concern. Profound questions also arise:

- Will we honor the "least of these"?
- Will we disdain the poor as "moochers" and "leeches"?
- Will the rich get richer and the poor get poorer at the present accelerating pace, or will we find some balanced policy where all give a little more?
- Will we live by falsehood or the truth that makes us free?
- Will we seek justice as well as privilege?
- Will we go on the warpath again—invading and occupying other countries—or will we seek enduring peace between nations and religions?
- And our women—will they achieve authority over their own bodies and have the right to contraception and abortion?
- And the immigrant strangers among us—will they be enemies or brethren in God and partners in the prosperity that we enjoy?
- Will women earn the same wage for the same work?
- In the wake of the "Citizens United" Supreme Court decision, will wealthy individuals and corporations be able to elect some and deny others by unlimited spending? Have the few beat the many?
- Who will be the next Supreme Court nominees and where will they take the country?
- Where will we head in the Middle East (Iran, Syria, Libya, Palestine, Israel, Pakistan, Afghanistan, Kurdistan, Iraq) China and the Far East?
- Where will we hope to move in the next four or eight years: stalemate or cooperation in Washington? Growing or shrinking deficits? Resurgent or regressing middle and working class?
- Will we move the nation from aggression to peace? Can we

reduce the military/security budget that has quadrupled in the last decade, and move toward peace and development?

- Will we find the heart to heal the sick, release the prisoners, bring good news to the poor, feed the hungry, attend to the widows and orphans?
- The epicenter of meaning and justice in the present political world is the Israeli/Palestinian conflict. Heal this and the war on terrorism is resolved. How and Who?

My Comment: As FDR said in his second inaugural address, "The test of our progress is not whether we add more to the abundance of those who have much; it is whether we provide for those who have too little." This passage alludes to John Calvin who said, in the sixteenth century, in a passage on Manna in the wilderness, referring to divine sustenance as analogous to economic provision, that "God wills that there be equality among us, that is that none should have too much and none should have too little" (*Commentary on Second Corinthians* 8, especially 1 Corinthians section, Ada, MO: Baker Publishing, 2007). The present election is not about economics and jobs, it is about bread—bread for the world. I will never accept the Marxian thesis of economic determinism. In this world, which is better understood not as a manifestation of human power and control but as the creation of God, the real issues are those of faith and justice, fairness and peace, not human ingenuity and power. The only human reality that is paramount—approaching the wonder and wisdom of God (Psalm 8)—is human freedom and responsibility since those distinctions arise and are sustained within the creative judgment and mercy of God. "In Him we live, move and have our being" (Acts 17:28).

Calvin perceived a special bond between rich and poor. In the divine scheme of providence, these entities are meant for the instruction of each other. He called this the mysterious intertwined destiny of *"les pauvres et les riches."* None are meant to have too much and none too little. The healthy are given health to care for the sick. The strong are given strength to uphold the weak. The old are here for the young and the young for the old.

The Hebrew Bible ends and the Christian Bible begins with the same words from Malachi:

> Remember the law of Moses, behold I send Elijah the prophet before the coming of the great and dreadful day of the Lord and he will turn the heart of the fathers to the children and the heart of the children to the fathers lest I come and smite the earth with a curse. (Mal 4:4–6; Luke 1:17)

A new world awaits us in science and technology, medicine and education, energy development. Can we break the gridlock in Congress and move together to help the nation and world? Cancer and chronic disease (heart and organ failure), dementia and mind failure, infection, public health and hygiene issues, all disorders of genetic or environmental origin, all lure our skills. The secrets of life and death tantalize our knowledge and lure our virtuosity in hope. All this from the One who "subjected the world to futility in Hope" (Rom 8:20).

Two

Excursus: George McGovern

Sunday, October 21, 2012—*George McGovern dies.*

We learned yesterday that Senator George McGovern had fallen into a coma and had been admitted to a hospice for the final hours of his life.

A graduate of our seminary, Garrett-Evangelical, for his ministry studies, and our sister university, Northwestern, for the PhD in history, George McGovern was a pastor, professor, politician. He possessed that deep history that we understand and call Shephardic. Senator McGovern formulated a concrete proposal for *jus post bellum* (justice and peace) at the end of war. In his book, *Out of Iraq* (New York: Simon and Schuster, 2006), one sees that his core studies and singular passion were bread for the world (see also his early books: *War Against Want*; *A Time for War/A Time for Peace*). His passions are not couched in theological language, per se, though it is implicit and often explicit in them.

McGovern teaches us why the United States we should have left Vietnam and why we must leave Iraq: Injury and death to thousands of American youth and hundreds of thousands of Iraqis, costs that will ultimately reach two trillion dollars, faulty *jus ad bellum* (e.g., charges of weapons of mass destruction and *jus in bello*—Abu Grahib; apocalyptic rather than reasonable rhetoric: "axis of evil"; "not for/against us"). McGovern also spells out values that ought to now determine our course of action and also, a way to get out of Iraq.

Though a big time loser in his presidential run, McGovern is one of my greatest heroes in American politics, right there with Jimmy Carter, James Madison, Abraham Lincoln, and Woodrow Wilson. All of them possess qualities that I hold dear. I flag McGovern as an exemplar of the cardinal values—justice, peace, regard for the "least of these." He was an inveterate peacemaker with strenuous realism. That his prescriptions in *Out of Iraq* are ignored by all the pundits and professors who write about concluding this war may provide some evidence for the veracity of his positions. I distill here his central points with comments on his implicit, though nonstated, theological presuppositions:

- *"The kingdom of God is among you" (or, peace with justice as status quo ante).*

  The historian and student of history's most important foundational text—Augustine's *City of God*—begins with the human yearning for and divine requirement of "Peace on earth, Good will among men." *Civitas Dei* (City of God) approximated in the midst of *Civitas Terrena* (City of Man) is McGovern's starting point. The pastor-politician seeks to reconcile warring parties. He demands truth in place of propaganda, justice, and mutual respect in the place of hegemony and exploitation; "getting on" rather than giving ultimata; working together rather than pursuing self-interest alone. He goes against all of the operative rules of politics, yielding to the politics of God and the good—the realm of God. His political theology is not highly conceptual Schlesingerian, Niebuhrianism, or Hobbesian Tertullianism; it is simple: "Love your neighbor as yourself" (Mark 12:31); "Do justice, love mercy and walk humbly" (Micah 6:8). These are straightforward Dakota ethics. —He had these verses placarded in his work room from childhood to (I would guess) his hospice room.

- *"The truth shall make you free" (or, Why did Al Jazeera so infuriate the American command?).*

  Northwestern University, in McGovern's day, was the home of truthful and thoughtful "free press" journalism. We struggle to make it so again in this age of corporate sponsorship/censorship of the media. There is something of the Quaker in McGovern—demanding truth in order to undergird strenuous social action. After 9/11, the American press and media, most studies show, were in the firm ideological hand of the White House and the war-justifying and war-prosecuting agenda. While that has liberalized slightly after the democratic election victories in 2006—it still remains the case, as I see clearly when I live abroad, as I now do on sabbatical in England. America's large recent-immigrant community and her (increasingly marginalized) intellectual elite had access to the international media, thanks to the liberty blessing of global electronic access. But the folk in the American heartland were left at the mercy of Fox News and the corporate networks where, it is said, media moguls with their Wall Street proclivities kept in place the "party line" agenda. Truth, Truth Commissions, and getting the story straight will be central to reconstructed jus ad bellum and jus in bello in the coming jus post bellum period. It may not happen at home, but it will be accomplished somewhere, and we will know about it.

- *"Let all the world in every corner sing/My God and King" (or, Who are the Iraqis?).*

Of the myriad array of excellences in McGovern's approach to JPB in Iraq, which hint of theological influences, I point to the esteem and respect he pays to the ancient and honorable people of Iraq. Here, in the ancient world of Mesopotamia and the Babylonian Empire of Hammurabi, some of the world's first justice codes were struck. Here, in the eighth century, in concert with Syriac Christians, a philosophical, medical, and theological heritage would spring from the bosom of Muslim culture. This culture would transform the still barbarian West and make the Renaissance, modern science, and religious learning possible. Not protecting the Baghdad antiquities are grievances that our side must face in the jus post bellum proceedings, along with burning Qurans, urinating on Muslim corpses, and dropping Osama bin Laden to the sharks with no reverence for the kadosh requirements concerning the corpse. Regrettably these desecrations will haunt us for generations. But then we are a people of rage, not reverence.

The larger conviction that McGovern is commending to the world in these pending proceedings is the integrity and dignity of all peoples and nations of the world, and the correlate notion of involving the largest possible international authority in settling disputes among these peoples of the world. In the book of the Acts of the Apostles, Luke the physician tells the world about a new postethnic, postparochial *oikoumene* (world house) that is appearing in the world through Jesus—dead, now risen—conceived as Christos (anointed Messiah), Logos (Eternal Word and Wisdom), and Kurios (Sovereign Lord of the world and its history). This new yet old, past yet future, arbiter within the world's domains, describes a theology of history and lands where God has fashioned "from one blood all nations to dwell on the face of the earth, has appointed the bounds of their habitation . . . that they should seek him and find him [for he is near to us all] . . . for 'in him we live, move and have our being'" (Acts 17: 26–28).

In this theology of nations (which I believe but have no evidence that McGovern subscribes, except that he is a graduate of one of the better "global mission" seminaries in the world), nations are bound together in one human blood-bond under one sovereign God of history. From this premise flows the requirement of mutual understanding and respect among nations. In this case, it means simply that we need to get to know them—their language, culture, faith, and feelings—and they us. In terms of the JPB issue, this means in the very least we must seek cosmopolitan analyses and answers to the issues, in terms of just war in particular, and do so with the widest, most global authority possible for resolution of the conflict. Though there is much to be said for national sovereignty, and the necessity of individual nations for tackling the issues squarely and decisively, we also need to enlist the UN, regional associations of nations, and proximate neighbors to help. And we must be willing to accept the authority of these cosmopolitan entities.

McGovern also helped the world see the futility, stupidity, and God-forsakenness in our supposed "divine mission" of deliverance in Vietnam. He was too good for this cruel world. In sum, McGovern's proposal rings with Christian theology and resonates with the themes of Christian global ethics. If Christ is the *Way*, *Truth*, and *Life*, then these three dimensions of his proposed policy deserve the support of those people who bear Christ's name in their own personal, ecclesial, and socio-political worlds. One who wrote more lucidly than any other of this new global understanding put it this way:

> Finally, brethren, whatever things are true, whatever things are honest, Whatever things are just . . . these things do and the God of peace will be with you. (Phil 4:8–9)

Good jus post bellum counsel!
Well done, good and faithful servant!

Three

Booklet on 2012 Election

and

Excursus: Theology of the Presidential Candidates

Here I insert my *Citizenship and Faith* booklet, which we used for election conferencing around the country: "Obama and Romney: Religion, Ethics, Citizenship, and Community" (A previously unpublished pamphlet by Kenneth Vaux: 2012.)

In the celebrated Broadway musical, *The Book of Mormon*, a kindhearted spoof is leveled at the rapid-growing American faith tradition poised to become not only a religious force comparable numerically to Jews or Muslims in this country but also a household word. The signature songs in this musical mockingly revel in the brash, latency-laden dialect of the *South Park* kids: "God Loves Mormons" and "You and Me (but mostly me)." The superficial theatrics of the show and the pyrotechnics of the religion itself seem to confront us with a new faith of blithe prosperity, manly confidence, and rather unbecoming hyper-Americanism. Critics say that Mormon temples in Africa and South America seem to shout "Crystal Cathedral"-ostentation and mammon. We're unsure whether we are dealing with a sect like Scientology and the "Moonies" or a serious variant of the Judaeo-Christian heritage.

But the story I wish to explore with you lies deeper than such speculation. Now, as Mitt Romney, the Republican standard-bearer, bears his well-concealed Mormon mantle (along with his passion for making money—lots of it), he tries to dethrone another political-evangelist who regrettably also seeks to distance himself from what society might regard as an equally unmentionable Jeremiad: liberation theology (see the new film, 2016), which is shrouded in an interfaith dream-coat of many colors. The religio-political fervor of this jabbing, heavy-betting boxing match in the Nevada ring between two heavyweight presidential contenders may be enticing to watch, but the portent it has for our nation and world history is profound. Religion and politics will address each other in unprecedented ways, and a cathartic and creative—but certainly cataclysmic—rumble is to be expected. This essay seeks to stimulate such a public inquiry.

On the eve of JFK's election in 1960, a feat thought improbable because Kennedy was a Catholic, his brother Bobby Kennedy commented that in thirty years a black American "could be sitting in your office." Twenty years after that portentous date, one esteemed American "Best Man of Letters" (Harold Bloom), conjectured that in 2012 the president might be a representative of the quintessential American religion—Mormonism. To ready ourselves for a repeat of the first or the initiation of the second, let us therefore review dimensions of President Obama's and Governor Romney's faith, political theology, and social ethics in policy and practice:

Faith: The religious identity of each pugilist

Political Theology: The political ramifications of the two persuasions

Social Ethics in Presidential Policy and Practice: How the national and international landscape may be affected

The Faiths of Romney and Obama:

Romney's Faith:

By way of introduction, in my ironic and irenic temper, I can do no better than to yield the stage to David V. Mason, a theatre professor and avowed practicing Mormon, writing in the June 13, 2012, *New York Times* (sec. A 23). Because of its theological acumen, and for the sake of this discussion, I cite, in part, from his Op-Ed piece, "I'm a Mormon, Not a Christian":

> Mormon doctrine is rigorously providential and predestinarian. God speaks directly to people and answers prayer. Beyond this it develops a theology of prosperity and of personal and political "chosenness."

> For the curious, the dispute can be reduced to Jesus. Mormons assert that because they believe Jesus is divine, they are Christians by default. Christians respond that because Mormons don't believe—in accordance with the Nicene Creed promulgated in the fourth century—that Jesus is also the Father and the Holy Spirit, the Jesus that Mormons have in mind is someone else altogether. The Mormon reaction is incredulity. The Christian retort is exasperation. Rinse and repeat.

Mormonism indeed is not Christianity, and does not need Christianity for authentication. It is an American faith and a faith in America. It may be seen not so much as a fourth Abrahamic faith but as an American heresy, perhaps an idolatry—perhaps the idolatrous heresy of "Americanism." Mitt Romney's early career entailed a draft exemption so that he could be a Mormon evangelist-missionary in France. By contrast, Obama launched his mingled career as a council of churches-commissioned pastoral worker—ministering to the distressed, laid-off steelworkers of Chicago's south side.

Of the fourteen-plus million Mormons in the world, most are in the United States. Like the sister nineteenth-century faith/life movements—including Christian Science, Jehovah Witnesses, and Seventh Day Adventists—Mormonism is a health religion. With a mandate of no "hot drinks" (tea and coffee), alcohol, tobacco, or other drugs, the Mormon faith has fashioned, through preventive care and a solidarity-based system, one of the nation's most effective health care entities. All this with an exuberant epicenter flowing from America's Dead Sea (Great Salt Lake) and the Mormon Tabernacle and its choir with her signature resonance of patriotic praise. Though not Barack Obama's Harlem Boys Choir, the Mormon Tabernacle seems to be the perfect venue for Kate Smith—though not Mitt Romney—to sing "God Bless America."

Believing that Christianity was living in "a great apostasy," Joseph Smith became the receptor of revelatory tablets that would show the way to restoration and redemption. One problem: The presumed words from heaven were actually well known early nineteenth-century spiritual texts. Like the Quran's precursors in the Arabic poetry of centuries preceding Mohammad, these words, received or borrowed, would become the Book of Mormon, sacred scriptures to which Smith added the "Doctrines and Covenants" and "Pearl of Great Price."

Though biblical conservatives cannot accept the Christian tradition's breadth of inclusion, the Mormon Christology is really not that far off base. Jesus, as the Mormon credo makes clear, is "God's first child," who comes and will come to earth to remedy sin. Jesus, John the Baptist and James, Peter and John all made appearances to the founders of Mormonism. Mormons believe in the cross-generational life of the soul as being pre-life persons who arise in the mind of God and eventually flow to an afterlife in the hallowed or haunted halls of heaven or Hades (Sheol). Those who remain here on this earth can coax the departed into heaven through the proper oblations and coins. Remember that God, for our sakes, though rich, became poor (2 Cor 8:9). Both Republican and Democratic conventions displayed this heretical flourish.

On the positive side, we find in this "get rich theology" (e.g., Wesley, "earn—save and give away—all you can" salutary impulses of freedom, free enterprise, and opportunity. Negatively, it brings about smugness and disdain, even imputing blame, condescending pity, and God forbid—lethargy and sin—to the weak and poor: the real woodcutters and water haulers of the world. Such respect for the true workers of the world is hard to stomach for investment bankers, buy-out specialists, and religious people of that ilk.

The doctrines of God and theodicy are paramount in Mormonism. God is particularly human, American, this-worldly and Jesuit (a Jesus Society). Unable to domesticate Yahweh as her sister faith—as the Jehovah's Witnesses did so easily—God became just "like us" and not "so Jewish, so unpleasant, so disobliging, so absent" (Bloom). (See James Wood's "The Misreader," in *The New Republic*, 5/1/2006, 24, regarding a review of Harold Bloom's *Jesus and Yahweh: The Names Divine*, Riverhead Books, 2006.)

Mormon anthropology expresses similarly bizarre notions. God has become man in order that man can become a god. In this apotheosis each male Mormon man will be lord over a star. In this strange doctrine of the saints we understand the remarkable god-like audacity of Romney who says with perspicacity and omnipotence that "I" will not allow Iran to have nuclear weapons. Such serene cosmic lordship cannot, of course, be mistaken or thwarted.

If, as I believe, the one God of Abraham, Isaac and Ishmael, Israel and Jesus, is the triune God; and if—as I also believe—that Scripture (Hebrew and Christian) holds that the three covenants—Isaac (Israel),

Ishmael, and Jesus are valid until the end of time, then the Mormon faith falls short of the theological requirements of iconoclasm, divine simplicity, and unicity along with the ethical requirements of love and justice. Mormons wrongly believe that they see the unseen God, know the unknowable God, and succor and are succored by the nonindulging God. They therefore mimic the heretical versions of truth and right among fundamentalist Jews, Christians, and Muslims forwarded in the nineteenth century and continuing thereafter. This departure from truth and justice in early-modern theology is chronicled by Karen Armstrong in *The Battle for God* (New York: HarperCollins, 2000). Modern Judaism, in this account, is, in some part, an American phenomenon. Christianity—in its evangelical, fundamentalist, even holiness, Pentecost version—is also Americocentric. And global Islam—certainly in her reactive Jihadist form—has to do with Americo-Israel and their various invasions and occupations in the world. The Mormon worldview, in other words, arises to political prominence in a particular season of interfaith history.

The faith that animates Barack Obama is similarly ambiguous and complex in etiology. When "Barry" moved to New York City as a twenty-one-year-old, he began to confess an unusual and idiosyncratic faith that is something of a mélange of familial disposition, Adam Clayton Powell, Dietrich Bonhoeffer (both ministers at Abyssinian Baptist/Harlem), and Jeremiah Wright. We start to see a divine political ontology that has the same fatal flaw as does Romney's Mormonism. God is reduced from mystery and rendered as a political idol. What follows is a telling text from *Dreams from My Father* (New York: Three Rivers, 1995) in which Obama recounts events shortly after he slept fitfully in a dark and trashy alley in Harlem, on his suitcase, on his first night coming from California:

> I might wander through Harlem—to play on courts (hoops) I'd once read about or to hear Jesse Jackson make a speech on 125th, or, on a rare Sunday morning, to sit in the back pews of the Abyssinian Baptist Church, lifted by the gospel choir's sweet, sorrowful song—*and catch a fleeting glimpse of that thing which I sought.* (my emphasis, p. 121)

Though moved by Bonhoeffer and his mentor, Reinhold Niebuhr, and therefore preserved in some orthodoxy and orthopraxy, Obama was first and foremost a politician (businessman), as was Romney. Barack quickly disowned his pastor Jeremiah Wright when the going got rough and, like Romney, always sought expedient testimony and was careful never to speak openly and candidly about faith, except in vague and universal terms. "What will sell" or "what will please our super PAC donors" becomes the God/Truth imperative. With both men, as with Saddam Hussein, the prayer rug is removed from the shelf—dusted off and used—especially when the press corps is at hand.

Since the faith of both candidates is all too human and flawed—in public expression at least—let us try to be "honest to God" and identify the subliminal reality that both men seek to honor. Such sublime and authentic *being* displaces inculturated faith—"Ludicrous twaddle" (Kierkegaard)—and comes to the fore "when one meets his Waterloo." This indeed may actually happen for one or the other presidential candidate in early 2013—in what is anticipated and called "The Cliff" (economic, political showdown [meltdown?]—with mandatory budget cuts slicing indiscriminately across the board).

The fundamental theological issue that arises with Romney's faith, and the political appropriation of God's being into his political leadership, involves how that faith converges with or diverges from faith in the God of Israel—in the one God of monotheistic, Abrahamic faith; in the faith of and in Jesus as Christ—the faith of the Bible, Christian confessions and traditions. Obama is more orthodox.

One widespread interpretation holds that Mormonism has morphed through its American inculturation within the puritan ethos. It has become something like an "Evangelical faith"—defined as the nineteenth-century "born again" Jesus (not Yahweh) religion. This is the new meaning of "Evangelical," rather than the Lutheran, Calvinist, or Anglican connotation of the sixteenth-century Reformation.

But this transfiguration does not seem to hold up, because Romney (and perhaps Obama) seem to hold the unbiblical doctrine of "American exceptionalism" and some fusion of faith with the American nation-state and "The American Way."

In Obama's case, he is closer to Christian orthodoxy by virtue of the influence of Islam and its iconoclasm ("no other gods"), and of black liberation theology as it extols rescue of the God of the oppressed: "One who hears the cry of His people and comes out to deliver them" (Ps 34:17). Romney can also lay hold of the history of persecution of his own people—Joseph Smith, after all, was killed by a Christian mob in Carthage, Illinois. Obama can retort that his own people—American blacks—are still enslaved in these United States of America, where the same portion of the population is now incarcerated and disenfranchised in 2012 as was the case in the 1860s, that is, the pre- and post-U. S. war of emancipation. Barack's people still sing "Lift every voice and sing" and "Let my people go." A large portion of black society is disenfranchised today by the combined force of district gerrymandering, blatant vote suppression, and the genocide of racial incarceration.

Our inquiry continues. Now we can begin to see the crux of the matter.

What kind of political theology arises from these two faiths?

What social ethics and political programs can be expected from these understandings of meaning and responsibility?

One caution: If faith is hard to discern, theology difficult to decipher, and ethics full of ambiguity, then politics cannot help but be highly conflicted. Indeed, arriving at a universal and harmonious politics (utopia) would be offensive and even dangerous. In a free and democratic setting, politics can prove divisive, eventuating, as we have seen, in a stalemate.

One example: At present in America and throughout the world, no one knows for sure whether economic healing for our fractured "body economic" requires austerity or stimulus, or some combination of both. Obama, a great centrist and compromiser, wants near-term invigoration and job creation, while seeing in the long run—after the sick patient is better—the need for disciplined curtailing of governmental spending and deficit and debt reduction. Prompted by his theology and ethics, the Romney camp finds the crisis rooted in too much government spending, while the Obama camp calls for Washington to reverse the decimating layoffs of state and local governments of teachers, police, firefighters, road and bridge builders, and garbage workers in order to satisfy the promptings of his beliefs and values.

Regarding nationism and nationalism as idolatry/legitimate belief/practices, Romney wants "boots on the ground" big time, to safeguard and further the destiny of his "sacred America." This is not interior up-building of the common good of the people but homeland security, anti-immigrant border patrol, military expeditions against "enemies," and the sustenance and fulsome funding of surveillance/attack bases around the world. For Joe Biden, the only sacred duty in America is to honor returning veterans and the war dead.

Obama seeks to wind down this sector of expenditure and begin rather to resource and replenish the public sector in order to invigorate the economy. This is in keeping with his theology and ethic of keeping the "social body" viable and strong.

Who is right? Only time will tell. At present all the nations of the world—most especially America, Europe, Russia, and China, but also the Americas, Africa, and broader Asia—are laboratories and test grounds of this particular matrix of political policies arising from one or the other conceptual matrix of faith, theology, and ethics. All over the world peoples are rising up like eagles or falling down like dominoes in rapid-fire frequency. Two great belief orientations—one stressing the unity and universality of God, the other the particularity and provinciality—are alive and well. In the end, theopolitics and ecotheology are about "my God" or "our God."

A word about transmission of policy-potent belief: Musical compositions from gospel songs to symphonies are political (polis) meditations. So are essays, poems, books, paintings and sermons, and the emergence, full bloom and collapse, of a red hibiscus. All these are vehicles inspiring us to transpose convictions into public deeds—parables. To be attentive to such proclamation-events, we must cut away propaganda, advertising, disinterest, and boredom. Only then, with the set cleared, can the drama of transfiguration occur and the miracle of political theology spring to life. Seeds need soil and water and sun to die and become transfigured into life. In the mercy of God, the world is forgiven and summoned into new life. Politics, if spirited, stirs the latent and moribund being and community into life. Theologically speaking, politics is a dimension of culture that is a dimension of Spirit. Politics rise within the life of God in the world.

SUMMARY OF THE DIVERGING FAITHS

In the opening episode of the HBO TV drama, *Newsroom*, broadcast on April 22, 2012, the anchor is being interviewed by an audience of college students. A young blonde coed raises the provocative and perennial issue: "What about our being the greatest country in the world?" The panel host assents, agreeing. The anchor objects:

> Best in the world? We sure used to be. We stood up for what is right. We fought for moral reasons. We struck down laws for

moral reasons. We waged a war on poverty not on the poor. We sacrificed. We took care of our neighbors.

A Sidebar on Health Care

Chief Justice John Roberts—a tried and true conservative—now appears on an Obama "Hope" T-shirt. The Obama health care reform bill—The Affordable Care Act—has been upheld by a 5-4 vote. Roberts joined the court moderates against the Scalia-led conservatives. The air waves exult with two strange messages: "I am Obama who cares" (Obama); and "I will repeal Romney . . . whoops! Obamacare" (Romney).

The historic achievement in this, the solitary advanced nation in the world that does not provide universal health care to its citizens, is more about John Roberts than it is about either Obama or Romney. It proves again that one party or other does not have the corner on what Paul Krugman antinomically calls cruelty or decency. Most pundits claim that Roberts was trying to safeguard the integrity and reputation of the high court, or protect it from the negative reputation incurred by divisive narrow decisions. Some even predicted that as it rapidly sunk in public respect that it was closing in on three strikes and you're out—after the contentious Bush v. Gore decision, in which it effectively named the president in 2000. To this was added the Citizens United decision (2012), which allowed big money and Super PACs the ability to buy elections.

A closer look at the court decision at the end of June 2012 showed that Roberts was more likely coming from an instilled theological and ethical heritage wherein he learned the moral genius of Catholic social teaching that states the needy, sick, poor, and old are our trust under God. Attending Notre Dame Elementary School in Long Beach, Indiana, and La Lumière Roman Catholic Boarding School in La Porte, Indiana, Roberts took to heart a tradition that rises above all expediencies—legal, economic, and political—in instructing our convictions and behaviors. In high school, Roberts was an excellent scholar-athlete with five years of Latin and a grounding in French, choir, drama, the school newspaper, and student council. Most likely he and his priest or sisters/teachers were steeped in the Catholic tradition's absolute insistence on honoring the poor, the workers, the sick the weak, children, immigrants, the old and dying—the "in as much, least of these." This training trumped demands for political expediency. It now remains to be seen how the "better angels" and religious orientations of Obama and Romney ultimately play out; for these two highly political animals could succumb to constituency biases and prejudices to do whatever it takes to get elected.

SUMMARY OF THE POLITICAL THEOLOGY OF THE TWO CANDIDATES

We are now ready to close in on our differentiation of Obama and Romney, and how their differing faiths might signal the ways their campaigns, policies, and presidential actions could differ. Though there is an enormous reserve of hatred for Obama by white conservative males and a significant upsurge of skepticism about Romney, both candidates are generally liked and respected by the general population as intelligent, competent, and faithful human beings. Practically speaking, it appears that both candidates are seen as good family men, religious leaders, persons of wealth with hearts for the poor, and persons of integrity. In our scan and overview of each, we must note that the faith formation of each candidate is complicated to discern and describe. It is difficult to offer predictions of what difference their faith might make to their presidency. Both are intensely private and nondemonstrative when it comes to a public display of faith.

Their respective political theologies and social ethics are also as tricky to identify. To assign these as predictive of varying behaviors is an equally difficult task. Admittedly, I am totally baffled when trying to anticipate how each will respond to the impending crisis in national and global economics signaled by Simpson-Bowles, or Paul Ryan, or Paul Krugman. Each offers contradictory prognostications as to what is coming in early 2013, and nationally and internationally we are at a loss to say whether the country needs austerity or stimulus efforts.

For example, in America and the larger world, which kind of hope would serve us better: laissez-faire and decentralized focus, or managed or centralized investment in the public order? Today, the Romney camp finds the "job" crisis rooted in too much government spending, and the Obama camp finds that this crisis is caused by the drying up of economic vitality and viability in the public funding of jobs, especially at the state and local level: teachers, police, firefighters, and especially in our scorched-earth policies and our lack of "earth stewardship" that has brought on global warming. Romney wants "boots on the ground" only in defense, military, and security policy; and Obama would prefer to curtail these spending priorities and use our national wealth to create jobs in infrastructure investment, innovation, health-care reform, and the buildup of the private and public employment sectors.

To the pseudo-theological questions, are you better off now than four years ago? Or are things getting better or worse? As Obama, Hillary Clinton, and John McCain knew in 2008; and as Obama and Romney know in 2012 (Reinhold Niebuhr gets it right) things are getting better and better and worse and worse at the same time. Utopic and dystopic visions and programs—dreams of heaven or hell on earth—both fail. Only slow and incremental, day by day healings and redemptions bring about human and divine progress and solicit efficacy in the Spirit. Only faithful, loving hope and resolute caring and justice in concrete instances in this world supply hope and amelioration of the world's pain.

Like Charles Dickens in *A Tale of Two Cities*, we are not sure whether we face the best or worst of times. With lines today blurred between truth and falsehood—veracity and mendacity—we don't know whom to believe. Take the economic sphere. Obama heightens his strengths and suppresses his foibles. Romney exaggerates in a similar fashion. Obama claims to have "created four million jobs in the last two years," ignoring that from day one of his administration to today the job losses approximately equal the gains. True, we aren't losing 700,000 jobs as in the closing months of Bush's presidency, but misconstrual and distortion of facts cause disbelief in both candidates. In Obama's favor, the precipitous increase in national debt touted by Romney has not occurred, though the enormous upsurge of debt under Bush is met by stupefying silence.

Adjusted for inflation, federal spending has actually remained flat during Obama's watch. A scan of the graph of the federal budget's spending increases and debt deepening since 1950 shows that the line has actually flatlined with Obama. But politics is rhetoric—a furious barrage of misinformation buries us, and no one or no news outlet will dare demand truth.

Truth is always the first tragedy when public and private discourse turns bad. The truth is always somewhere between Fox News and MSNBC. With the departure of Walter Cronkite and Eric Sevareid we are left with Rush Limbaugh and Bill Maher, so with the Prayer Book we can only plead that "the truth is not in us."

How, then, ought we to live in a time when all semblance of decency and integrity has disappeared and only coarse disrespect and profuse falsehood remain? How do we live in this fallen realm of rhetoric, propaganda, advertising, and similar distortions? To preserve any civility at all, citizens must see through the cloud of fabrication—one made so much more insidious by Citizens United, Super PACs, and the possibility that the wealthy will take down some candidates and put others in place, as happened in the 2010 intermediate-term elections. All portend ominous danger for democracy in 2012.

Will one candidate be able to outspend his opponent two to one, five to one, ten to one? The essence of democratic "freedom to vote," which America affirms and monitors around the world, is now threatened right under the nose of Lady Liberty. With such economic coercion, an American patriot hides his money in Bermuda, the Cayman Islands, and Swiss banks; and a Nobel Peace Laureate pulls the trigger on civilian-killing drones and tempts the world into cyber-terrorism. The pot calls the kettle black.

Living with integrity and honesty, justice and truth requires that we see through the accumulation of falsehood and wrong. Today, the president is accused of deception in the "gun-running case" and the governor of concealing funds in Swiss banks. Where is truth? No one will dare say, contending that all we have—at least under the conditions of political existence—is half-truths and opinion.

The president gives papers to 800,000 immigrants to live and work in this country, and he asserts the ethical axiom of equal pay for equal work. Romney asks how we will pay for this new expenditure. Obama asks that we continue tax breaks for the "working, middle class," and Romney asks for the same extension for the top 2 percent, neither making provision to pay for the trillion dollars in cost. The poor man's president says that he favors the right to marry for gays; and from the shadows of his own tradition's flirtation with polygamy, the rich man's president finds this to be anathema, while knowing the Semitic and Hellenic, the holy and rational, grounding and bearing of that word. Without either candidate having the grace to compliment the other, at least for the other's willingness to serve the common good even at great sacrifice to their own wealth, we are left with ragged straw men. The dignity of every person before God is left in tatters.

Having sown to the wind, we are reaping the whirlwind. According to Harold Bloom, both Southern Baptists and Mormons—though sublimely inspirational—are, in the end, Gnostic (imaginary), Americanistic (idolatrously nationalistic), treacherous, and self-aggrandizing. In practice, Preachers Land and Wright, Preachers Joseph Smith and Romney, and even the black churchly rhetoric of a totally inculturated Preacher Obama, all practically follow the mischievous words of Joseph Smith in his "Wentworth Letter" of 1844:

> We believe in the literal gathering of Israel and the restoration of the ten tribes . . . That Zion will be built upon this continent ("at our rallies"?) [author note: my addition]. That Christ will reign personally upon the earth and that earth will be renewed and receive its paradisiac glory. (Quoted from Harold Bloom, *The American Religion*. New York: Simon and Schuster, 1992, p. 84)

In profuse and vain imagination, we have abandoned the radical and demanding God of Israel and Jesus, and have made ourselves God while remaking God into our image.

MACROCOSM AND MICROCOSM / CHURCH AND STATE

Obviously, I am not wedded to either presidential candidate or either political party. As one who seeks to be a man of God, I seek to find a truth and goodness that transcends partisan interests. It is no easy task to appropriate concrete principles from the "transcendentals" of faith and love, justice and hope, peace and gentleness—values that originate in the divine order—into "practicalities" in the secular arena, Still I remain convinced that the political order is profusely theological, though awareness by operatives and observers of this parameter is negligible. At the same time, the "divine order" by its very nature is proclamatory and prophetic, seeking secular instantiation and engagement.

Harold Bloom reflects in *The American Religion* that Mormonism and African American faith are "varieties of the 'American Religion.'" In the imagery of William James in the *Varieties of Religious Experience*, these both reflect the salutary force and destructive pathology of American cultural religion (p. 46). We therefore further explicate the faith system of our two candidates.

NOTES FROM MY DIARY

Sunday, July 8, 2012. "I awake in a feverish cold-sweat. It is probably bodily, mental, and environmental as it is 95 degrees outside. Such inflammation has often been the instrument for me to see things more clearly than I can when in a placid state. Here's what I see in the current events of Church and State. As the saying goes, 'as go Presbyterians, so goes the nation.' On this Independence Day weekend, pundits predict that the candidate who wins Ohio will win the election. Right now Obama leads polls in Ohio by 50.1% to 49.9%. If Rob Portman is named GOP Veep, this narrow ratio may reverse by .2 %. Maybe then the Supreme Court will have to call the election as it did in Bush v. Gore. If Romney wins, his honeymoon may be short-lived with a congressional revolt in 2014, as happened to stop Obama in his tracks in 2010. My view is contrary to the shibboleth of the pundits. I'm sure that the real issue is not the economy and jobs. This "Marxian hermeneutical etiology" never was determinative. What is going on is fundamentally a matter of world-view and theology.

"The Methodist quadrennial, now reflecting its Afrocentric belief axis, has moved against gay marriages and ordination, the Presbyterians have backed off, and the Episcopalians have comfortably moved forward with standard liturgies and vows.

"On the issue of divestment to affirm Palestinian rights by censuring Israel, the same 50.1 to 49.9 razor edge has gone with Israel—reflecting either the blatant Islamophobia (especially Hamas and Hezbollah) in America or the fear that divestment would provoke Israel to bomb Iran, setting off the powder keg in the Middle East. Again my point—we are not dealing with economics but with biblical and theological convictions. Our only hope for comprehension and amendment of ways is theological idol-bashing and recovery of lost faith and ethics. This essay offers some hints at that redirection.

"Romney scores significantly higher with married women and Obama with single moms—what did we expect? Presbyterians affirm the patently erroneous view that from the beginning of creation "marriage was between one man and one woman"—a cultural invention in the last 100 years of the "nuclear family"—again by 50.1 to 49.9. Pittsburgh and Columbus—*Church* and *State*. Non-political theology is non-biblical and non-theological. Our faith, as Bonhoeffer and Jesus witnessed in their martyr deaths, must be worldly—confronting the 'powers of this world.'"

LOCAL OUTCOMES FROM A GLOBAL PERSPECTIVE

From the global perspective, it must be pointed out, Presbyterians and Methodists—along with Anglicans for that matter—are preponderantly

African faiths. United Methodists number twelve million over against some thirty to ninety million Africans, if we include all in the Wesleyan and Holiness (Pentecostal) family. In Congo, one of our mission fields, there are twenty million Presbyterians over against two million in the United States. Blacks have quite different beliefs from whites on issues like fidelity, family, freedom for gays, and so on—and we are now a one world family. African Christians are also more afraid of Muslims than are their European and North American counterparts.

One other demographic from these cited assemblies has bearing on the assimilation of these observations. At the Presbyterian General Assembly, the 333-331 vote showed youth and clergy on the losing side and older white laypersons on the side that prevailed. This seems to accord with political demographics at present. Take Texas: in one or two more elections, it will be a Hispanic majority state—even with district gerrymandering and voter suppression. Anglo majorities can only last a few more elections. So the handwriting is on the wall, though the ancient regime will hold on tenaciously to its privilege.

These observations on the global church and state seek to show that political policies are derivative of and deeply reflective of fundamental beliefs. We can now bring to conclusion this comparative theological profile of Obama and Romney and sketch, in outline form, the practical positions and programs of each candidate that radiates from his particular underlying worldview and ethic.

GUILT, BLAME, DROUGHT, AND FLOOD

As the national elections draw near, the sitting president is blamed for every calamity in the world: from the global economic crisis that stretches from Beijing to Boston to the reality that it hasn't rained for two months in Chicago. He is blamed for the price of gas, but the dramatic turnaround must be credited to the governor. If we still had the sheer delight and terror of attending Obama's home church, Trinity UCC, and hearing the brilliant biblical messages of brother Jeremiah Wright, then we would be talking about how all of the world—be it political, religious, economic, and geological—was crying out a plaintive, birth-pangs moan of agony (see also Romans 8) as the redemptive impress of the Spirit of God met the resistance of the rebellion-bound world. As the psalmists and prophets resound in protest to the injustice and disregard of humanity against earth, fellow humanity, and Godself, the fish of the sea, flocks of the air, and fields of trees, howl like the "oppressed creature" (Rom 8:22).

One of my fellow parishioners recoiled in horror when I mentioned the name of the Reverend Jeremiah Wright. "I heard him shout, *God damn America*!? That is blasphemy," he said to me. And, no doubt, sooner or later, some Super PAC fat cat will make a TV ad depicting this insidious preacher spoiling the worldview of the innocent young black social worker. But these words of Wright's had simply reminded him of the tenor of apocalyptic and prophetic texts in the Bible, and the fact that God blesses and judges all nations on earth—especially those who consider themselves chosen, and those who misuse their might and wealth to harm the poor and destroy the peace. Yet he still found it inconceivable to entertain the possibility that God could damn such a great people like us. So we swelter away, in part because we have warmed the globe with greenhouse gasses, and because we despise the poor and sick as we luxuriate in our wealth and health. Perhaps these words were brought about in the justice of God by our presumption of goodness. "How Great Thou Art" has become "How Great We Are," and wind, rain, and fire obscures a "still small voice."

Soon President Obama will be assailed and accused of guilt by association with Pastor Jeremiah Wright. During his community organization work, Obama had praised the pastor. "It was this capacious talent of his—the ability to hold together, if not reconcile, the conflicting strains of black experience—upon which Trinity's success had ultimately been built" (*Dreams From My Father*, New York: Three Rivers, p. 282). Soon Obama will be reviled as he was in 2008. My apologia then and now is that Wright gets it right, and he is squarely in the center stream of black liberation preaching. Present day Nigerian megachurch prosperity preaching, by contrast, is fully heretical by its refusal to accept the demonic allure of riches, so fundamental to the prophets and Jesus' message. Wright is "spot on," and for that reason will be widely reviled in the new American ethos.

Wright would become the pastor to the Obama family's coming to faith, and he will once again keep silent and not rise to defend his mentor. Despite this, Obama will get at least 50.1 percent of the vote even though he has been charged to be the cause of every evil—the world economic collapse, draught and disease (HIV), flood and pestilence, the job crisis, big government. Actually, employment has improved during his watch, and the overwhelming loss of jobs came from loss of public sector employment over the last three years—especially teachers, police, firefighters, and first responders—mostly at the state and local levels of government.

In succoring and favoring the rich in tax policy as well as with a multitude of other favors (e.g., pilfering the people's money in dishonest banking activities, bad loan practices, funding futile wars, and the like) wealth has been concentrated in the miniscule few while the "middle" and "working" classes disappear. The very wealth, which God intends for the uplifting of his oppressed peoples, disappears into the black holes of virtual cyberspace and into the accounts of the hyper-rich.

SUMMARY: COMPARATIVE CHART OF POLICIES TO EXPECT

The President must be a servant and statesman. He or she is called to (1) extend *peace*, (2) establish *justice*, and (3) edify *environment*. These are the ethical callings of the shepherd. In specifics, this would mean the following:

Economics

B. O.: Let taxes rise slightly for those making more than $250,000, including small businesses; simplify tax code; strengthen regulation on banks, mortgage companies; encourage economic growth by policies that encourage middle-class business initiatives; job training for the poor; and work with the private sector with incentives to create jobs. He could also allow sequestration to bring about mandatory budget cuts across the board, perhaps excluding the budgets for military/security expenditures?).

M. R.: Extend Bush tax cuts to all income levels; offset deficit/debt increase by cuts of public services, public employees, "freebie" programs (college loans, food stamps); enhance deregulation, especially for Wall Street and big business; more laissez-faire approach to all business; decrease size of federal government; and perhaps shift more economic activity to states. He could also adopt Paul Ryan's economic program.

Health Care

B. O.: Affordable Care Act—Obama-Care ("I do care"). A major commitment to make health insurance available to "almost all" Americans while reducing runaway costs. Maintain Social Security and Medicare by cutting administrative red tape and redundancies, and retaining private delivery systems and insurance companies.

M. R.: Maintain private and corporate structure business model for health care delivery, saving Medicare and Social Security, perhaps by privatizing. Poor without insurance should be cared for by private philanthropy, state provision, reducing malpractice cases, cross-state insurance pools.

Security/Military

B. O.: End wars in Iraq and Afghanistan; maintain strong security structure at home and around the world (with bases); build on Clinton and Bush strategy of emphasizing drones and cyber-sabotage activity to confront security threats; support Israel while keeping relations with the Islamic world, China, India, Pakistan, and allies in Europe and Asia; support development and partnerships in Africa and South America; partner with private sector—Gates, Buffett, (adding some of the very wealthy mischief-makers—e.g., Edelsohn) to combat disease, feed the hungry, supply fresh water, respond to disasters.

M. R.: Greatly expand American power, supremacy, and security through unprecedented funding, and pay for it through cuts in education, welfare, and social programs; eliminate foreign aid (except to Israel); cut Planned Parenthood domestically and internationally; prosecute the war on terrorism with Manichean fervor and intensity; stimulate global trade freedom and resist other nation's tariffs while enhancing our own.

Environment

B. O.: Lessen dependence on foreign oil; regulate and tax multinational energy companies; push on natural gas, wind, solar, geothermal with careful environmental protections. The government's role is to encourage private sector; fund initiatives not possible in the private, for-profit realm; and regulate for public protection.

M. R.: Expect ecological responsibility from entrepreneurial and corporate sector; allow the free-enterprise dynamic full sway.

Both go for the gas.

Education

B. O.: Education is a centerpiece of his vision and commitment implemented by his Chicago buddy and one-on-one hoops partner, Arnie Duncan. Emphases is on teacher excellence recognized by better remuneration; tests deemphasized while preschool prep, parental involvement, corporate adoption, and ready access to higher education (trade and academic) are emphasized. The rapid decline in performance of American scholars in comparison to other countries is a major disgrace to all three Harvard grads—Barack Obama, Michelle Obama, and Arnie Duncan—and the rest of us. Good teaching has autonomic power in bringing interest and accomplishment even to the most desperate inner-city, rural, and international kids.

M. R.: Dismantle the Federal Department of Education as well as teacher unions at the local level. We might expect him to accent greater family involvements because married moms seem to go for him at 60-plus percent. He also might be expected to see greater value in parochial and Amish (Hutterite) education. His family with many model children is encouraging. Perhaps missionary activity might be encouraged to offer habitat for humanity and social justice witnessing as well as door-to-door evangelism.

Immigration

B. O.: Advocate full equality and civil rights for LGBT persons, including option for consecrated unions; offer papers for the undocumented children of immigrants, thus allowing this population opportunities for work, military service, and relief from harassment; oppose voter suppression targeted at minorities; and offer comprehensive immigration reform in keeping with McCain, the Bush brothers, and many conservatives.

M. R.: Support a pathway to full citizenship, because this is an item of importance to the business community; and be tough on border security, especially as business picks up after Obama, should he lose the election even though he rescued America and the world from the Bush-era economic crash.

Four

Itinerary in Ohio: October 2012

THE DIDACTIC USE OF this pamphlet occurred in the fall of 2012. As I did in the 2008 election, before I was laid low by a serious illness (benign prostatic hyperplasia, or BPH), I visited churches and synagogues, schools and colleges, homes and shopping malls—even crowded city sidewalks in Pennsylvania, Indiana, Wisconsin, West Virginia, and Illinois. Here is a scan of my fall 2012 itinerary:

Tuesday, 10/2: Drive by Defiance College, Bowling Green, Findley University—throw out a few brochures and put the hex on them.

Wednesday, 10/3: College of Wooster—Meet with campus ministry, religion professors, students in student center, workshop in college church (using pamphlet, "Theology of Candidates").

Wooster is an excellent college in a state with unprecedented numbers of first rate small liberal arts colleges. Leaders emerge in the professions and in the general public, intelligent and ethical leadership in the nation and world. Great audience for dialogue on "Faith and Citizenship."

Thurday, 10/4: On to Pennsylvania—Neighbors and family, Amish community, Bob Kranack, our house sitter. In 2008, I did citizenship seminars in western PA.—Grove City, Allegheny, Slippery Rock, Westminster, Mt. Lebanon, Pittsburgh.

My natal place and the roots of our family for 200 years. The epicenter of my family church—Presbyterian. We began our ministry here and raised our family at Hemlock Haven. A lovely stone home, trout streams, place of respite, insight, and peace. A swing state and historic home of the republic and her founding. My dispositions as a theological scholar are formed on this landscape. I am some Andrew Carnegie—engineer, entrepreneur, builder of local libraries, Presbyterian preacher. I am some Ben Franklin and Benjamin Rush—virtuoso, inventor, skeptic (as required as prohibitive and imperative of Torah/Way of God), healer (of plagues and animosities with Amerindians), and constitutionalist (in state and church, vis-a-vis John Calvin).

Friday, 10/5: In some ways, my best day. Left Janey in the dark at 4 AM. Drove up through Sharon, PA. Ohio border and up into Youngstown. Parked in the lot of the public/university library as dawn broke. I met two obviously poor and struggling inner-city black students. (Youngstown is a dirt poor, depressed, Appalachian city—having lost half of its population in the last four decades—yet surprisingly vibrant and full of life.) I gave them the brochure. They were intrigued. I found them hopeful and hardworking. One was getting ready to form an online business to help young persons in the inner city gain reading and organizational skills. I wandered around the corner and deeper into the Youngstown State University campus. Then the fun began. An Obama bus was there, one of a series that was transporting students and professors out into the city to canvas neighborhoods to register people to vote. I met the conveners who were college students from Beverly, Illinois; from South Chicago. They were on leave to work in the Obama campaign (an impressive ground game) with as much, if not more, enthusiasm than we saw in 2008. They told me to stand upon the hill near where the bus was parked, hand out my informational pamphlet to each person, answer questions about the two candidates: their philosophies, theologies, ethics, politics; questions about Mormons and Jeremiah Wright and Obama's faith; questions about their view on the issues—the economy, war and peace, abortion and contraception, woman's issues, the poor, middle class and working class; views on the Middle East—Iran, Syria, Islam, Judaism, Christian theology and traditions. Then, these thirty boarded the bus and radiated out throughout the city to canvas, to register, and to vote. And the next group formed. Today, as I write this memoir, they do the same thing with different celebrities and different scholar-consultants. I made it clear that I was there on my own funding and that despite my obvious support for Obama, as an academic I would seek to be fair minded and nonpartisan. I convinced all the leaders (while I was there at least) to take students out to work or to register or to vote—whatever their persuasion. I sustained this neutrality, hard as it was, as I had always done as a professor, in all the venues I found on this itinerary.

After a heart- and tummy-warming bowl of New England white seafood chowder, I took a few more cycles; returned to the library; listened to Eva Longoria, the beautiful actress, make her persuasive pitch: "Are you registered—why not?"; and then headed west on Route 322. Now I found what seemed to be the longest flea market in the world—after Les Puces in Paris and Mercados de la Ciudad de Mexico. I couldn't help myself, refurber that I am, from picking up a rusty, worn, woman's, blue Schwinn bicycle that I believe had sat out in a Fred Sanford–type front yard with old fridges and mowers for fifty years—sporting sufficient rust and disregard to prove its vintage.

As evening neared and Cleveland loomed far in the distance, I knew I needed to stop and find lodging. I went in to the local Methodist church—always playing the Garrett Seminary card—enjoyed two brownies at their bake sale/bazaar. But no rooms at the Inn. I swung through Hiram College—enjoying the Friday evening football prep activities (against John Carroll, I believe)—distributed a few pamphlets and settled for a flea-bag motel in Streeterville. The night was rough, even sickening. But this, I found, as I struggled to see and breathe, was not from Route 322 and the west Cleveland environs but from my premature shortened night with my old campaign stomping buddy—my cousin Janie Craig Kober—a seventy-plus-year close friend—who had just acquired (rescued) a family of seven cats. Even a loading dose of Sudafed could not save me from the three orange tabbies, two grays, and two jet blacks—one named "Kenny." Even though I loved the little guy, whom I crushed by sitting on top of him on Janie's Archie Bunker–style TV chair, as I introduced her to our favorite political commentator on MSNBC—Rachel Maddow—by 4 am, I was out of there.

Saturday, 10/6: Arrived in Cleveland, coming in from the eastern suburbs, then driving down the long Martin Luther King–like drive—Euclid Ave.—to the University Circle. I checked in at the Glidden House—an extraordinary B&B right in the midst of the great churches like UCUMC (University Circle United Methodist Church)—the "Oil Can" Methodist Cathedral where one of my gracious hosts, Dr. Ken Chalker, held forth and Covenant United Presbyterian Church, where the inimitable pastor, Bert Campbell, has fashioned an amazing "progressive" church that is the focal point of superb preaching. The environs were full of exciting cultural activity, interfaith ministry, and lively student ministry in the middle of Cleveland Clinic, the Art and Music Centers, Case-Western Reserve University—the cultural matrix of one of the world's great cities. Here I would hang my hat for five days, finding numerous occasions to ply my trade in my long contemplated ministry of Faith and Citizenship. This was the best I could offer to this international epicenter of world society on "such a day as this." How the world would go would probably be decided in this NE corner of the "Buckeye State."

Sunday, 10/7: Henry Curtis IV met me at the Glidden House at 9:30 am in his silver Explorer—adequately capacious for his lovely wife and five children. We had visited intensely by phone for two months, renewing our friendship fifteen years after he was my student at the Seminary. He warned me before we proceeded further: "Dr. Vaux, I'm a Republican. My wife [Ebony] is president of Republican Women. I have a day job as director in the Cuyahoga County Voting Department. We scope out and hunt down voting fraud and voting suppression. My bosses are the mayor, two Republicans, and two Democrats." They later gave me hints that they were supporting Obama. I told them my purpose was the same as it was when I taught him decades ago: to help your scholars become careful readers, thinkers, writers, and speakers, regardless of party or affiliation. I've long known from my studies in post-Hitler Germany that no political party could perfectly embrace truth and goodness. Henry had set up a worship service with me as preacher and co-celebrant at Eucharist. He was an AME (African Methodist Episcopal) ordained Pastor, now working on a Doctor of Ministry degree at Methesco Seminary in down-state Ohio. After two hours of worship, he invited two other churches to join us for a light lunch and a seminar with the now infamous pamphlet.

I preached on 1 Corinthians 13 and, feeling like my old Anglican, Lutheran, and French Calvinist cantor-self, I sung the lesson, then added Hal Hopson's wonderful paraphrase of "The Gift of Love" (Trinity Hymnal, Carol Stream, IL: Hope Publishing, 1972). My message followed the following witnesses:

> Hippolytus in the third century—the first catechesis service litany for the early Church: "What is your intention toward widows and orphans?" (*Hippolytus: The Doctrine of the Faith,* in Hermeneutics

series, Ed Phillips, Minneapolis, MN: Fortress, 1995.) The first principle of *Christian Ethics.*

Thomas Aquinas—the father of all Christian theology in the modern world, Catholic and Protestant:

"Scripture and all truth is given for the building up of one another for the '*Common Good.*'" ("On Government 1267," in *Summa Theologica*, Aristotle's Ethics.)

In his first inaugural address, President Obama—one deeply shaped by biblical truth—spoke of the Love chapter of 1 Corinthians: "When I was a child, I spoke like a child . . . when I became a man I put away childish things" (1 Cor 13:11). If the president has learned anything in this tumultuous and frustrating first term, it is this lesson of "coming of age." He must now face "principalities and powers—evil powers in high places." Simple rhetoric and vague ideals will not get him through "times such as this." In the portentous days of Queen Esther, external forces in Israel's world combined with interior weakness. Only obedience to God and righteousness among people could pull the nation through crisis. America faces such a crossroads.

After the worship, we held a one and a half hour workshop. The congregation clearly understood the implication of worshipful public action in this time and place. Blacks and Hispanics, women and the poor, young people and progressives—the full wisdom of Queen Esther—would be needed to rise up in concert and stand up to evil if the ominous force of near 70 percent of angry white males was not to lead this nation into paths of danger. Such an election had not been seen since the time of the United States Civil War.

The good day ended with a reception-discussion at the home of Carol Roe—a religious leader at Covenant Presbyterian, health care expert in dialysis care, grassroots political organizer—assembled to discuss the convictions and policies outlined in the pamphlet. Friends who gathered seemed to appreciate the value of the little book for use in their religio-political work. The insight I took from this group is that there is no easy and obvious connection between faith and helpful political activity. As we learned sixty years ago in the civil rights movement, indeed, in the sad record of religious history, organized religion is as often a force for evil as it is for good. Especially at this time in American history, distorted faith is woven into the Christian right/Tea Party political substance. Good faith and derivative ethics is also the moving force in all public life.

Tuesday, 10/9: After a day of rest on Monday, another fascinating day rolled out as a continuation of Sunday. I met with Rabbi (Pastor) Ben Gohlstein, the Baptist pastor in the neighborhood of (Dr.) Henry Curtis IV's Mt. Moriah AME. He and his social worker wife—two remarkable leaders who joined the Curtis couple as spiritual bulwarks in the neighborhood (Hood), city, and nation. Ben and I hit it off immediately on Sunday—both having roots in Judaism, his in Middle Eastern/African, Jewish culture; mine in sixteenth-century Switzerland. He kept his name. The best I could do was to come out of the closet and own (with pride) my own ancestor in Reb Josef Rosenberg, whom Sara discovered in her family research in Europe, we both having suspected the hereditary connection from my dad's olive oil complexion after his mother, Ethel Stuart Vaux.

Both pastors were well connected with social service, hunger ministry, social justice concerns, and the national/international networks of the African and African American church—the vital heartbeat center of global Christianity in our time—a time such as this.

After Sunday's workshop, Ben immediately set to work arranging for me to be the keynote preacher at Tuesday morning's meeting of the United Pastors in Mission meeting at Mt. Sinai Baptist Church at 7500 Woodland, in the city of Cleveland. Some thirty pastors—all black—gathered under Rabbi Ben, who then asked each pastor what he had preached on this past Sunday. Then another powerful baritone pastor led one of the signature songs of the black church. The occasion brought tears to my eyes and joy to my heart, as if I was back at First Church of God at Dajae's funeral in Evanston or Second Baptist with its lively choir and preacher or Trinity UCC with Jeremiah Wright in the dock or in Hattiesburg, Mississippi, in 1964 in John Cameron's clapboard church when I was asked to pray to the rumbling resonance of humming and amens. This, before we started out to protest voter suppression of blacks in the Delta—soon to be thrown into the city jail for a week. (See my memoir #1, *Ministry on the Edge*).

The gathering was a concerted, Bible-based church, dedicated to civil actions that the world has come to know through the works of Bishop Tutu, Nelson Mandela's uprising against apartheid in South Africa,

Gandhi's satyagraha (peace force revolution in India), and the civil rights struggle in the American South beginning in the 1950s.

They checked in on the success of measures to stop the voter intimidation and suppression—a fight against local, state, even national government officials who were in place since the Tea Party takeover of politics in 2010, and aided by the U.S. Supreme Court ruling of the Citizen United decision, which opened the door to a nefarious and major co-opting of public life and politics by extraordinary corporate and individual big money. Were the buses and cars ready and available to take "souls to register and to the polls"? This, remember, was taking place under the threatening Tea Party billboards throughout the "hood," warning "We're watching you—voter fraud could cost you 50,000$ *or an 18-month imprisonment!*" We were back in segregationist Alabama, apartheid South Africa, or the ghettos of Warsaw.

Several lay pastors from the Teamsters "ministry" department in Detroit told of what they could offer. NAACP lawyers were around to provide legal aid. They asked me to provide the biblical theological background. Ben and the other leaders of the group cautioned me to "go soft" on some of my political-ethical beliefs that "wouldn't preach" here. Social justice and poverty issues were okay—gay issues, Islamic references, and critiques of military "would not preach." They all seemed to know my oeuvre and, of course, I ignored their counsel. I gave my talk with which I began this diary—sprinkled with local occasion and color. We preachers and politicians only have one sermon.

Wednesday, 10/10: United Methodist Church in the University Circle. Dr. Ken Chalker arranged a very exciting evening seminar at the "Cathedral." My seminar was the second in a series of election programs. Ken led the first evening the preceding week with a discussion of a new book that argued faithfulness to the Bible texts required one to take a certain "right wing" political text. Ken showed that this argument was not only wrong but that Scripture actually set out the opposite direction. It was good to see that at least a few "white guys" and a good number of white women had more progressive and idealist/ethical convictions. I attribute this to the grassroots sense of justice and concern for the poor and "the least of these" embedded in the traditions of the Wesley brothers. The proclivity to side with the simple and poor, to reach out to those oppressed, sick, old, and denigrated—the despised of the world—has always been a trait in the tradition, even in the modern American scene where the yearning to seek success and the prosperity gospel became a god even for "the people called *Methodists*," as with the Jews, where the faithful and observant always remembered the longstanding "marks" seared into the flesh and piety of their own people. After the program, I took my leave of Cleveland—wishing it Godspeed and drove bleary eyed but content through Akron, Canton, and down into mid-central Ohio, finally to collapse at 11 PM to rest contented in Cambridge, Ohio—seven miles from Muskingum College.

Thursday, 10/11: Muskingum College, New Concord, Ohio. I arrived at my alma mater at 8: 30 AM. Our good old Volvo wagon had made the complete aforementioned tour. Another eight-to-nine-hour trip awaited, including an overnight within 100 miles of home. But we were "Rolling Home." The old chapel had been carefully refurbished and maintained, and the campus had been rejuvenated, reinvented, and carefully stewarded toward a usable future even during the past six years, which were a profound economic challenge. Muskingum had become a more pedestrian place since I won the campus oration contest there some fifteen years after George McGovern had done the same at Dakota Wesleyan. Teachers were being trained as they were in my day sixty years ago. Not such good liberal arts—theology/philosophy, pre-med, pre-law, pre-min, pre-politician, pre-professor ethos as half a century ago. Now, more vocational studies—pre-commercial, low-level business careers. The world had changed here in mid-south central Ohio—Wheeling, Marietta, Zanesville. We were no longer Wooster, Dennison, Kenyon, and Oberlin Colleges. We were now Muskingum University. No longer Christ College, Cambridge, or Merton College, Oxford—we were now Muskingum University. I remember when I spoke at chapel, say, thirty-five years ago. I said I would have been proud to have our kids come to Muskingum. Not really. They went to the University of Chicago, Harvard, Oxford, and the Sorbonne. Still, I loved the place and was thankful for being nurtured into a BMOC at this beautiful place where the teachers were excellent and interesting, the students were decent and friendly—where everyone said *Hi!*—and where a lasting and satisfying philosophy/theology of and for life was inculcated. So I reminisced.

Ohio, I discovered, was a class act: the plethora of fine, small Christian colleges for small Christians. Though frayed around the edges—Youngstown, Steubenville—river towns and river rats, it still exuded a dignity and character: deep south and cultured (and not so cultured) north. Winesberg, Ohio, and Sherwood Anderson's resilient humanity and good sense, especially if it resisted the Romney fabrication that things were getting worse and it was the black guys' fault and we white guys could surely do better than a black, Muslim, socialist. But God forbid if we sold the nation and the future of our children down the river. Even John Glenn, thoroughgoing conservative patriot, was a true Democrat, a son of the William Rainey Harper, Robert Montgomery republic. I think today as I write (and as a bizarre "perfect storm" of slashing heat and tropical torrent, along with blowing snow and bitter cold, threatens not only the eastern coast, reaching Halloween fingers back even into Ohio), if this good state sells this country, follows Boehnor and Alabama, Palin and Arizona, Sununu and Texas into a rage-state of angry white males—full of replete mendacity, to buy such a fabricated falsehood—I will flush her down the toilet in a moment. Tea Party—no way! It was like the rabid band of rich, mean Methodists who called themselves circuit riders (or the Presbyterian lay committee). I agree with Halford Luccock: "I'd like to see those fat guys on a horse" (Luther's larcenists on swivel bank and business chairs and black suits).

My host was Chaplain-professor Will Mullins. I brought the message at his chapel, visited with students at lunch, and spoke to his class in Christian theology. The hymn he had chosen was accompanied by a fine pianist professor—a student of the Schnitker's. The opening hymn after the moving candle lighting was Sibelius's *Finlandia*, an incisive insight into my message: "This Is My Song." From the United Methodists, stanzas 1, 2 are by Lloyd Stone, and stanza 3 is by Georgia Harkness, the first great woman theologian in America, who taught at Garrett—my seminary.

Reconstructing my ruminations, Georgia Harkness's verse, stanza 3, is a salient masterpiece of Calvinist theology. It reflects the wisdom of her book on John Calvin. The key points are that this land is God's and ours—this nation is our heritage—received from God. All nations have special beauty, memory, and future—as with our nation. Other lands have "sunlight beams and clover" as ours does. "Skies everywhere are as blue as mine." Two theological notions interplay here. One is Jesus' teaching that the rain falls and the sun shines on the just and unjust (Matthew 5:45). This is exceptionalism extended to all nations. The Lord is the Lord of all earth's kingdoms, for "The earth is the Lord's and the fullness thereof" (Psalm 24)—and in words understood as I write during the cataclysmic weather events of October 29 and 30 in North America:

He hath established it upon the seas" (Ps 24: 2). All we can say and pray in cataclysmic times which seem "biblical" in their moment is "Thy Kingdom come on earth—thy will be done."

I loved the music at Muskie, Chanticleer—a new group in the world but soon one of our best a cappella ensembles—appeared in this chapel as part of an excellent series of performances, speeches, and musical events. I sang in the college choir directed by Woody Pickering, a prince of a maestro who introduced countless amateur singers into a high class secular and sacred repertory. Biologist Clement Dasch, botanist "'Wild Bill'" Adams, and chemist Sy Vellenga shaped my love of science and an ethical vision for science that has been a leitmotif of my conviction and passion ever since. Speech, oratory, and debater profs Golden, Johnson, and the Laytons supplied the nascent preacher and the writing/speaking public intellectual. Historians Fiske and Sturdevent, literature profs King and others, philosophers Dykstra and Short, Rife and theologians McLelland and Hutchison and the arts professor Louis Palmerand, coach Bob Burkholder—all showered me with exquisite learning and personal care. I will ever be in their debt and thankful for their mission as scholar-teachers. For me it was great that as a modest athlete, amateurish musician and rhetorician, irrepressible dilettante, I was able to flourish multidimensionality because of these splendid faculty persons, supportive parents, secondary schools, churches, and fellow students. *Gott sei Dank* to one and all!

Friday, 11/2: Milwaukee, Wisconsin. It was hard to drag myself one more time onto the campaign trail. While it was still dark, I loaded up my booklets and headed for Milwaukee. The Kenwood Methodist Church welcomed me. I parked the loyal Volvo wagon in her lot and spent the morning across the street at the Campus Union. I had driven by Bert's home on Stowall Street. I wondered if I should stay through tomorrow when Obama will be in town. Just hours before, Senator Russ Feingold had spoken. Recalling his work for fair and true elections, Feingold helped the students see how they could get out the vote; how they could counter the considerable efforts of the Romney campaign to suppress the vote, to intimidate and discourage voters; and how they could counter the massive influence of big-money on elections, which Romney had endorsed. Those Tea Party forces had undermined Feingold's own distinguished, sterling career. Feingold, we recall, pioneered campaign finance reform with John McCain in those golden days before the Republican Tea Party congress decided to undermine every Obama effort to pull this country out of its deep malaise that began in 2006.

Friday, 10/26: Id al Aydah/Day of the Sacrifice. Lambs are ready for sacrifice in the kosher/kayrut butcher shops here in Chicago, as well as in Mecca, Dakar, Gaza city, and Alleppo, Syria—indeed all towns and cities on Earth where the reviled and revered "people called Muslims" dwell. In the latter war-torn city, where much of the ancient tradition of Islam began as it arose from the cultures of Judaism and Christianity, government fighters crawl through the rubble door-to-door like rats as they do in nearby Homs. While this violent search-and-destroy mission grinds on to exterminate the apostate enemy, attacking the equally fervent insurgency of the "liberate Syria" forces, in the Id, around the poor swath of humanity on the equatorial band around the center of the world, they roast the lamb and carry it to the poor and neighbors, while asking for forgiveness and renewal of life. Meanwhile, the antithetical destruction of life ensues; the obverse of the Mosaic, Messianic, and Muslim command *Choose Life!* In Afghanistan, a suicide bomber and dozens of innocents are blown to bits and a fragile cease-fire brings eerie silence in Syria. Two months ago—in a Eurocentric and American holiday called Labor Day—International Workers' Day, May Day by another name—I reflected on this very sacred/secular celebration. The liturgy of God's special ones in the world—the poor and oppressed—was on my mind while the word remained unmentioned in the campaign and debates except for a staged washing of a few pots in a soup kitchen by VP candidate Paul Ryan. At least he tried!

Five

Homily: Come Labor On

September 2, 2012: at Second Presbyterian Church, Chicago.

September 9, 2012: at Highland Park Presbyterian Church

—A Homily by Ken Vaux.

Texts: Psalm 28: 4–9; John 6: 26–32; James 1:17–27.

Hymns: "Come Labor On"; "God is Working His Purpose Out."

WE FIND OURSELVES TODAY in the important holiday season of Harvest Day, Labor Day, church rally day, post-rummage day, back to school day. It's a "hope springs eternal" day. Paraphrasing Shakespeare, kids with shiny faces and carefully stocked backpacks and lunch boxes "creep off unwillingly to school." The pressing questions of life now change as we frolic from Vivaldi's summer to Auden's autumn—"are we there yet?" From the back seat of the car, now becomes "when do we start 'Christmas shop till we drop?'"

Autumn is resolution and redemption time . . . new beginnings . . . kids off to school . . .

Where and how does faith come into this pastiche of worldly business? What meaning can we find here? We can start by seeing that in all faiths, work is worship. Liturgy (*leiturgos*)—what we as a faith community are now offering to God—is work offered to the One who alone is worship-worthy—worth our work. This is the one creator/redeemer God who stepped into world history. Just as the history of the world is the history of God, so the God-story is our becoming story. John put it this way: to do the work of God is to believe in the One he has sent.

What does this mean? Surely, it must mean that God is doing something here and now—in this world—with and through us. God is Emmanuel; God has come into our life to sweep us into God life; and God is working. Zion, then Golgotha, then the empty garden tomb is a bulwark, a mighty fortress, a stronghold of care and comfort, a base station from which will proceed redemptive work for the world, a lighted path through all darkness, the warehouse of all good and perfect gifts that come down from the Father of Lights. My teacher at Princeton, Bonhoeffer's friend Paul Lehmann, said that the key question for faithful folk was "What is God doing in the world to make and keep human life—human?" Two responses at the church door captured the congregational response: "This has nothing to do with faith" and "At last a Bible-based sermon that deals with our life in the world."

The Bible sees the labor of men and the double labor of women as stigmata of the fall, which also means that these endeavors are windows of freedom and opportunity. All three faiths of Abraham see three besetting sins defacing human life and dishonoring God—our maker and redeemer. The three snares of Beelzebub—that evil one within and among us—are (1) idolatry—serving "false gods," (2) immorality—wrongful, hurtful treatment of others, and (3) riches. This latter temptation is problematic since we also believe that God prospers the work of our hands. As we work out our salvation with fear and trembling—God is working his purpose out. John's gospel says that God's working exudes manna in abundance into the world. It is good substance provided for the life of the world. It is meant to be shared and distributed equitably. We misshape it and turn it into mammon by craving it more than God, by grabbing it for ourselves—stealing, hoarding, hiding—while not sharing. Look closely at what is happening with God's abundance poured out into the world as manna.

Economists, who do not like manna/mammon language, have an indicator called per capita GDP. This is the amount of wealth accruing to peoples in the world per year, per person. In Africa, it is $500 per annum: $1.50 per day. In China, it is $5,000 per capita/per annum. In Singapore it is $50,000. In the United States, it is $100,000. Ninety-seven percent of Americans come in under $250,000 (although Senator Chuck Schumer says you can't live in New York for less than one million dollars), and few small businesses can cash out at $250,000. Three percent of Americans come in at *more than one million* dollars—this includes a lot of Presbyterians. The top 1 percent are at 10 to 100 million dollars and above, and they surf in loopholes. We may be seeing for the first time in American history that this small sector of millionaire/billionaires able to control elections.

A billionaire named Mr. Adelson says it will be worth 100 million dollars to him to bring down the current president, Mr. Obama—and a frightful multi-billion dollar mendacious advertisement now unfolds on television. In America and abroad in many places, we find an accelerating yawning gap between the very rich and the very poor as the working and the middle class slowly disappears.

Idolatry, injustice, and riches—the snares of Satan—are hauling in the storied Jesus fish who spit up coins in the Sea of Galilee while congressmen skinny-dip and while we neglect the message of the loaves and fishes. Look up our oldest scriptural texts—the Dead Sea Scrolls and the Aleppo Codex—fortunately rescued from the rubble of these now beleaguered sites. These treasured Scriptures are full of such warnings.

Bring it down to real people. Today, in one school in Florida, thirteen children are homeless, living in cars—and this is typical. They wash up and brush their teeth in a gas station, then go off in their car to school—guess we could call it home delivery. One of our colleagues in liturgy today gave me one of my favorite impressionist paintings by Caillebotte—workers scraping and sanding the floors of some privileged Parisienne. The title of the work is from Matthew (6:34), "sufficient for the day is its own pain." A few weeks ago we heard that on that particular day half of the populous nation of India, 700 million persons, were without power, without light, without water—that's 10 percent of the world's people. If anyone throws at you the dishonest " welfare/work" bit these days, just have them cruise the streets of every city in the world at 5 am and see the blacks and browns—poor men and women—going to their work and toil. So much for the myth of we privileged white guys still in the pad.

John is talking about this in his treatise on light, life, and bread. Where's God? What's going on? What went wrong in this world destined to be as full of the glory of God as the waters cover the seas? How have we bent it so out of its glorious and generous shape?

The Holy text finds a very clear imperative on this matter. Here, in this world, God's work entails our work: heal the sick, care for the homeless. It's called neighbor care. Ancient Iran invented "house health" that the Chinese took over as barefoot physicians. Someone of every village—a natural nurse—who knew everyone by name would tend to perhaps five hundred people in the parish, offering manna, medical, and economic knowledge. Care must be effective—food, jobs, health care, learning, gardening, and water access. Only neighbor care can help when lost livelihood leads to lost health. In America this becomes diabesity: no fresh fruit and vegetables, the called ambulance, the ER, the collection agency, the heart attack, exacerbated diabetes—ending in exorbitant national expense—now 17 percent—of that composite GDP we just noted. All because we can't muster the faith and hope to care. When neighbor care disappears, when we are told to fend for ourselves, the world becomes a luxury liner beached on some drought parched and thirsty land. This is how the Bible describes judgment: a frightening realm where we cease stewarding the world garden and rebel against the divine kingdom of love and reciprocal care, and forfeit a flourishing and sufficient creation. By contrast, everywhere we choose to live by neighbor awareness and help—house health, home nursing, house work, house church—here people are upheld from falling through the cracks into the oblivion of anonymity, and the day's pain can be absorbed into God's work, his hand bringing a friend to your hand and his own free and ever-abundant manna.

To bring it home, obviously we're talking about the nineteenth century CE in human history and modernity in the history of God. The era was described most acutely by a prophetic Jew, grandson of rabbis and the son of Protestant believers. Marx and Engels write, "A spectre is haunting Europe and all the powers of old Europe have formed a holy alliance to impede any remediation of this spectre—Pope and Czar, French radicals and German Police spies. Religion wants to understand we want to change things" (Martin Bailey, *Van Gogh in England*, London: Barbican, 1992). Vincent Van Gogh—a contemporary of the German comrades, one who sensitively painted the poor and struggling workers—visited an art exhibit in London devoted to this theme. On one work of the poor huddled in a dark and dangerous London alley, he saw a text from one of his favorite authors, Charles Dickens. It said this: "Dumb, wet, silent horrors. Sphinxes set up against that dead wall and none likely to be at pains to solving them until the general overthrow." Dickens speaks here not of the proletariat revolution but of the God redemption—working out its purpose in the world. So let us now close and invoke benediction and peace on one another with other words of a great nineteenth-century philosopher/priest—an Anglican who became Catholic and founded the Oxford movement, in part in response to the fact that Catholics better maintained a sacramental solidarity with the poor and didn't give in to the Protestant prosperity gospel. So as we close our Labor Day meditation on work, world, word, and shalom, the words of Cardinal John Henry Newman take on new meaning: "Lord, support us all the day-long until the shadows lengthen and the *busy* world is *hushed* and the fever of life is over *and our work is done*. Then in your mercy grant us a safe lodging, and eternal rest and *peace* at the last through the Lord Jesus Christ. Amen" (English Book of Common Prayer, 1152).

REFLECTIONS

The sermon caused a stir: much discontent, some "I'm ready, let's go," and a broad midrange frenzy of apathy. It frames its themes in an interfaith context, which is hard to get our heads around. The Id is a pan-Abrahamic faith postulate (see Jon Levenson's *The Death and Resurrection of the Beloved Son*, Yale). All three faiths celebrate sacred sacrifice as woven into the very fabric of Earth history and *A History of God* (Karen Armstrong). These faiths, though each having distinct and unique integrities and provenance, radiate from one crux of meaning. This unicity of meaning is inescapable, given the unity of the one God of Abraham and the unity of the creation of that one God. The world cannot be fathomed apart from God nor can God be discerned and adored apart from his world. In sum, we either live and move in God or we cease to be. Whenever we seek meaning and value—in our individual and corporeal existence—world and God must enter our contemplation and faithful action.

As I write this reflections portion of text, on this autumn day of flaming color—of life and death—Chicago's radio station WFMT plays Mussorgsky's "Pictures at an Exhibition," driving our personal and collective minds to Tarkovsky's *Andrei Rublev* and the iconographer's great mystic depiction of the divine creation and our human co-creation and on from there to the mind of God. Thornton Wilder reminded us that that was the location of Grover's Corners (*Our Town*, 1938).

Six

Superstorm Sandy

First Reflections: Monday/Tuesday.

OCTOBER 29 AND 30, 2012, begin with three pictures. Our three-year-old grandson, Ehren Curry, stopped over when he returned from school at Latin School in Lincoln Park—Chicago's North Side. He was exhausted and agitated as he and his sister, Aislinn Moira, hit the house, wanting something to eat and some drawing paper. The little man was also looking for his tiny action figure, Spider-Man. As grandpa continued to be glued to the weather and the MSNBC news channels following the most ominous weather event of my life time—"Superstorm Sandy"—"Little Man" went into his not-unexpected major meltdown. Was it a "Perfect Storm"? It involved an enormous tropical hurricane with unprecedented wind and water surges, meeting a freak snow storm along the "Appalachian spine," sliding westward and meeting another unusual low pressure front. But my opening reflections as a biblical theologian riveted on three off-frame pictures. "Little Man" was bewildered without his tiny "Spider-Man" superhero. His psyche, no doubt, was like a herd of buffalo listening to a coming sand storm with hoof and ear while it was still hundreds of miles away, and so he could not help melting down.

The second and third scenes were along the devastated Jersey shore, just miles from my sister and family in Kenilworth, New Jersey. We talked with her by phone just hours before the telephone connection broke down. We were comforted that she and my brother on the north shore of Long Island had acquired generators against the dreaded nemesis of a power outage. In the morning, I watched pictures of two water ducks gently floating in seeming oblivion to the troubled surge waters in the streets of towns along the Jersey Shore. Then, in picture three, there were three black labs frolicking in delight in the rushing waters and blowing winds. Meanwhile, millions were without power. Regular institutions—schools, stock markets, perhaps even national elections—were closed, delayed, perhaps rescheduled. Meanwhile, as an eighty-story crane dangled over downtown Manhattan like a Japanese paper sculpture, the blessed creatures of God's good creation—ducks and duck-hounds—went about their regular serene routines, and a "Little Man" collapsed into blessed sleep in his little bed.

Meanwhile, his theologian grandpa meditates through the cataclysmic night, seeking cosmic, theological, and ethical meanings. Having to teach and comment to various audiences each day—the teacher goes to work and invites you into the meanderings of his mind and heart. I start the reflection with what great drama calls comic relief in the three pictures. The dimension of the comic interrupting the tragic is the gift of a philosophical/theological point of view. Faith and ethics are open to the possibility that the sacred touches and interrupts the secular. We therefore are completely empirical as well as fully religious if we accept the possibilities of the judgment and mercy of suffering, death, and transfiguration. We use words like "biblical proportions" and "Stormageddon." Three civic officials, governor and mayors, full of "fear and trembling"—the metaphor great literature and common sensation of all sorts uses for a confrontation with terror and thrill—speak in their fumbling words of the holy and the Holy Other intuited in these moments.

Governor Chris Christie standing stolidly at the epicenter of Elijah's holy mountain of wind and fire speaks of a shephardic commitment to his sheep in ways that transcend his more customary partisan stridency: "I don't give a damn about election day," he wisely opines. New York Mayor Michael Bloomberg sets aside his Wall Street corporate room demeanor again to offer the warnings, admonitions, and consolations found in his deepest theological impulses: "We will move heaven and earth to help our people who need help." Interesting phrasing, as if those potencies were within our power. The mayor often frequents black churches in Brooklyn where he is no doubt reminded that "faith can move mountains" and can even stop the subterranean springs . . . Then there is black mayor Lorenzo Langford of Atlantic City—sin city with its magical boardwalk to heaven or at least Hoboken: "The sixteen deaths up and down the Eastern seaboard of this storm are sixteen too many—but we have been spared and are blessed."

> God is our refuge and strength, a very present help in trouble. Therefore we will not fear, though the earth be removed, and though the mountains be removed, and though the mountains be removed into the midst of the seas. Though the waters thereof roar and be troubled, though the mountains shake with the swelling thereof . . . Be still and know that I am God. (Ps 46:1–3; 10)

Seven

Sunday in the Park, or a First Corinthians Study

First Presbyterian Church, Evanston, Illinois.

Last night was Halloween, "All Saints evening," the day of the dead in many languages. From the vibrant life and color of autumn, we slide into the stillness and death of winter (see my memoirs #2: *While I Have Being: Winterreise (Winter's Journey)*. Our favorite newsman/commentator, Rachel Maddow, who provides our daily "evening vespers," speaks of her costume for trick-or-treating. "I'm in my Halloween costume—tall, dark, lesbian pundit in dark jacket and blue jeans" (MSNBC, November 7, 2012). The issue of gay and lesbian persons has been lying quietly under the radar for months except perhaps for the few rabid homophobes who today blog that Atlantic City has just felt the furious wrath of the judgment winds of Jehovah God blowing Superstorm Sandy onto the Boardwalk of harlotry, debauchery, and buggery–perversion and inversion! I melt when I see a five- or six-year-old girl cry—especially Aislinn, my granddaughter. This one little dear, Abbye Evans, was riding in her mom's car, listening to NPR. She got out and started crying. "What is it?" she was asked. "I'm tired of Obaminy and Rominey [sic]". She wept for us all. Hateful acrimony seems to be the human condition. Even animals are not as chronically malevolent and maleficent. In last year's Academy Award film—Terrence Malick's *Tree of Life*—a gigantic tyrannosaurus happens upon a tiny relative along a rippling stream. He approaches, lifts his big foot to stomp, pulls it back, then trots away and the little guy lives to see another day.

We humans seem more prone to hiss and stomp to "others" in violent hatred—and then to extinguish the gift of life.

Human violence traces a complicated pathway from thought to will, to speech, then act. Our American experience is frightfully replete with interpersonal hatred leading to attempted rub out. George W. Bush took down Al Gore, and then John Kerry. Obama took out John McCain in a cascade of destructive outings of Bush (orchestrated by his handlers) to which the good man surrendered as political necessity. Now Romney returns the favor with a downpour of mendacious attacks on Barack Obama.

Then there is the disdain and violence of angry white males against women and their rightful sovereignty over their own bodies. Senate aspirant Todd Aken parrots words of "legitimate rape" and in Indiana, Richard Mourdock unconscionably utters that the conceived baby of violent rape is "intended by God."

A pastor says wisely and gently that "to believe that God would choose to impose a pregnancy on one whose most basic bodily agency has been violated is . . . blasphemy against God's great care for those in need."

I'm intrigued by the theological underpinnings of such "othering" with intent to harm. In wrongful belief, we feel we need to anathematize others in order to separate belief from apostasy, righteousness from unrighteousness, Christ from Satan.

"Ken Vaux does not speak for me," say many of my parishioners and students. "He believes in full human and religious equality and rights for gays and Muslims." "God believes that we should be separated to retain 'Holiness,'" they contend. Strangely, we never ask whether Scripture and the will and purity of God requires such outing and marginalizing of one another. But we push our violent temper and action forward as onward Christian soldiers.

I traced this church-based drama last year on our congregation's study of 1 Corinthians. Here is an excerpt of this tracing, followed by my larger contextual essay:

> Our congregational study on First Corinthians—involving preaching, teaching, and community learning took a dramatic turn this week. A major meeting—requested by some constituents and agreed to by the Senior Pastor—Ray Hylton—was convened to explore issues arising in today's church pertaining to concerns raised by Paul in his letter—especially sensual licentiousness, even unspeakable violations—incest and temple prostitution, apostasy

and false worship. For our pastor and numerous members of our congregation, the discussion of homoerotic sexual activity took front and center even though in my view it was only part of a list of distorted behaviours—part of a cosmic darkness and Fall—one disputed today by most Bible students as having anything to do with the modern phenomenon of same-sex preference and derivative relations of fidelity within this community. Nevertheless, on this night, we confronted this one intensely provocative issue to us today—both from the side of felt threat and victimhood—homosexual liaisons and relationships.

In the twenty-first century—when church bodies vote to approve ordination to ministry to these brothers and sisters in Christ and the spiritual celebration of conjugal relationship in sacred places and when the public order is approving gay participation in martial and marital public policy—these issues intensify their provocation for some. Some say, with unbecoming disdain for gay and lesbian persons, things like, "We don't want *them* to teach our kids in Sunday school or preach from our pulpits—certainly not at the insistence of government or presbytery." This fear is pleaded in trembling voice. As one person blurted out to me amid tears: "Would you want your daughter to marry *one*?"

From the more inclusive perspective, persons ask, "Can't I even bring my lesbian sister, who has been a good Christian and faithful partner for thirty years, to Sunday service without hearing deeply wounding comments? Will our children, who may happen to be gay, hear harsh words about who they are in Sunday school?"

Such discourtesies are rare, and although our evening conference had more civility and seriousness than this banal chatter, the same underlying anxiety was evident. The pastor asked someone to show him any passage in Scripture where homosexual relations were condoned. Many of us wondered if there were really—on close, open-minded read—any passages that actually condemned faithful, monogamous homosexual relationships. In any case, Ray articulated his view that "gay" sexual activity was proscribed by the Bible from "cover to cover" and that gay sex "was of the same order as the biblical sins of pride, lying, drunkenness, greed, and so on"—matters for repentance and recovery of normative being, willing and acting. And in this case, he inferred "normative" to mean heterosexual being and activity.

Though a man of science, he did not find veracity in the notions of biological (even God-given) homosexual orientation. Even if this did really exist, he said, it was up to us to seek the power of the Holy Spirit so as to avoid putting the propensity into action.

The man is obviously well loved and respected, and his authority and intelligence are honored. In my view, I also will follow him into the gates of hell, which appears—in the worst moments—where we may be going. If I were permitted to speak (I am, as a minister and member of presbytery, not of the congregation), I would have said, "Don't abandon this good man and leave the church. After all, he is right on 90 percent of the issues—serving the poor; advocating women and children; advocating peace, not war; reconciliation, not confrontation; and opposing graft and corruption." Even with this blind spot, I would have opined, "*He's batting .900*—not bad in Chicago."

The latest mutation of position in the Presbyterian denomination—of which this particular congregation is a part and Ray and I are ordained pastors—is one of allowance for congregations to either marry or not, and to ordain ministers, elders, or deacons or not. This Calvinist denomination, which political philosophers say provides the belief and ethical basis for democracy in the world, is thus confronted with a particular challenge. The church can teach toleration and inclusivity, but it can't mandate it. Lutherans and Anglicans—even Methodists—should they ever get around to it, are Episcopal polities (bishops) and do not have the troubling exigencies of local freedom and minority protection amid majority rule through lay representative governance.

So it seems that when Ray chooses to highlight this minor theme from the panorama of sins Paul (and the Levitical holiness code) named, and when we ask whether this concentrated attention raises in some minds whether we actually welcome to our faith family such persons and even their advocates, the issue at hand seems to be whether we can still welcome this cohort of persons in church and celebrate their ministries in our midst or whether gays and their coreligionists should seek another church home. Would such hospitality offend the sensitive consciences of what appears to be the majority of the church body—especially the "biblical fundamentalists," self-designated "evangelicals" (which technically means not "born-againers" but Lutherans and Calvinists), and others of our sisters and brothers (especially newcomers) of tender and vulnerable faith?

Approaching the issue from the side of those singled out as the object of our approbation—can we maintain a milieu and atmosphere that includes both parties to the debate, rather than banish one side or the other to create some imagined purity? This posture of abiding the presence of each other while we all struggle for what Paul calls the "unity of the body of Christ" (Eph 4:1–16) seems to be what the majority will of our denomination seeks. There is to be no coercion from one side on the other but amity in the Spirit. Will it work? Can a conservative opponent of inclusivity be at home in the Fourth Presbyterian Church of Chicago, and can a progressive proponent of inclusivity find a spiritual home in the First Presbyterian Church of Evanston? Framed in Jesus' words, which formulation will we follow: "he who is not against us is for us" (Mark 9:40) or "he who is not for us is against us"? A world of difference!

If homosexual life is seen as incompatible with Christian life and/or if both camps claim to have biblical grounding for their convictions, can we ever expect to find peace?

Allow me an illustration shared last evening by British friends from Cambridge: "Imagine Ben Britten and Peter Pares—faithful partners for forty years—producing some of the greatest theological gifts [of music] in our generation, for example, 'The War Requiem,' where Peter joined with Dietrich Fischer-Dieskau in the stark octave spread duet on the Abraham-Isaac son sacrifice of the 'Beloved Son,' now referring in the Wilfred Owen's WWI poems to the sacrifice of sons and brothers on the Verdun battlefields. To condemn their gay union would be morally outrageous."

We all agreed.

CORINTH AND OUR CONGREGATION: A SEARCHING CHURCH FINDS DIRECTION IN AN ANCIENT LETTER

We move now to the outlines and text of our devotional 1 Corinthians study included below and in the following:

Introduction: "Veni Creator Spiritus"

I. A Divisive Body in a Fractured World

II. Wise Enough To Be Smart? Chapter 1

III. Milk and Meat: Holy Fools in the Divine Nursery and

Cradle of the World, Chapter 2

IV. Porneia and Passover: Can Impurity Be a Public Sin? Chapters 3 and 4

V. Love and Law: Marriage and Body, Chapter 5

VI. Conscience and the Needs of Others, Chapters 6 and 7

VII. Self-Denial, Sacrificial Love, Remembrance, and Parochial and Public Witness, Chapter 8

VIII. Received "Tradition," the "News of God," and Our World Watch, Chapters 9 and 10

IX. The Greatest Love Song and How It Preserves the World, Chapters 11 and 12

X. Stigmata, Resurrection Logic, and Cosmic Transfiguration, Chapter 13

INTRODUCTION: "VENI CREATOR SPIRITUS"

This work grows out of several experiences:

1. Tracking our pastor's sermon series on 1 Corinthians, which Dr. Ray Hylton sees as a charter for the Christian faith and good meat (and milk) for the faith-life of a congregation. For my part, this is the latest phase of a career-long practice of teaching and preaching in the local church. My specialty, and the orientation of this report, has been faith and the public order. For nearly fifty years, I have spoken and written widely on the matters of Paul's epistles—idolatry and injustice, sexuality and morality, health, marriage, life and death. I have offered my poor counsel by pointing to divine wisdom and authority as much as that is humanly possible before the *one* mystery "whose thoughts are not our thoughts and ways not our ways" (Isa 55:8).

2. Therefore, upon entering the 2012 election year makes it incumbent on me (and irresistible, of course) to address the theopolitics, economic theologies, and ethical issues that have become so profuse in our national and international life. The Bible concerns itself with the personal and congregational—the local, national, and international, indeed, cosmic

dimensions of life in the world—under God. As Harvey Cox often said, "Biblical religion is not only about the inner life and life after death."

3. In the award winning documentary *The Congregation*, a Methodist church in Philadelphia struggles with a new pastor to whose ministry another challenge is added: the unexpected disclosure that the assistant pastor is lesbian and is in a faithful relationship with her partner who is also a beloved part of the family of the destabilized and fractured congregation. The denomination, the United Methodist Church, based in the United States, but also in Africa, has not yet resolved its posture on the acceptance of homosexuality and the symbolic issues of consecration of gay relationships and the acceptance of ordination of gay pastors, further complicating the anguish and division of the congregation.

Our Evanston congregation finds itself, in our own season of ecclesiastical and political transition on these same matters, engaged in the study of a charter biblical, theological, and ethical text of this highly provocative and deeply felt subject: Paul's first Letter to the Corinthians. This author—a biblical theologian, pastoral associate in that congregation, and ordained minister in that "Presbyterian" denomination—also leads the Corinthian study, an educational adjunct to a five-month preaching series on Paul's epistle. Meanwhile, our own Presbyterian denomination has authorized ordination and sacred services of covenant and consecration, even as President Obama and the Republican aspirants to his job play with the issue and states accept or deny gay marriage. I myself have been involved for forty years in the denomination's to and fro on this signature issue, for example, as an author of the 1978 landmark minority report that discountenanced ordination to ministry of avowed, practicing gay persons. Over the years, with the insight provided by the struggles of church and society, and sharing the personal pilgrimage of hundreds of persons called to ministry, I have come to a position of acceptance and celebration.

4. Further complicating the matter, my own penchant is to do biblical studies in an unprecedented way, i.e., through interfaith hermeneutics, which looks at the way that a "Golden Chain" of Midrash (Scripture commenting on itself) is forged—alluding back into Hebrew Scripture and often even yielding insight from Islamic Scripture that often borrows from its parental faiths: Judaism and Christianity. In a reading that seeks to be

comprehensive in the most expansive sense, here I follow the widespread practice of "Scriptural Reasoning" (SR), which reads the three Abrahamic Scriptures as parallel cognates. I also follow Ken Bailey, Middle Eastern exegete—as one who is familiar with the Semitic tongues after decades of teaching in Egypt, Palestine, and Israel (and fluent in Arabic, Syriac, Coptic, and Hebrew)—and his brilliant book, *Paul Through Mediterranean Eyes* (Downers Grove, IL: InterVarsity Academic, 2011).

The Bible concerns itself with there and then (e.g., first-century CE Corinth/*Sitz im Leben*/historical study/exegesis) and also here and now (isogesis/hermeneutics/interpretation). Even when I preach or teach the lectionary, I sometimes lead out with the past (text) or the present (our life situation). For example, "taking innocent blood" (Deut 27:25) or Syrian or Lybian defense and security forces killing their own people or Americans mandating "abortion." Actually, I believe in the woman and family's right to take responsibility for incipient life in her own body, and I believe that family planning and contraception is a biblically acceptable mandate of stewardship of the body. I work daily as a theologian of the church with the Bible in one hand and the newspaper in the other—a protégé of Karl Barth.

5. I am moved by the sheer theological power and perpetual relevance of the Corinthian correspondence. As in Romans, Paul understands, I believe, that he writes as a "Spirit-guided" prophet and "apostle" (Gal 1: 11–12). Paul knew perfectly well what was meant by "apostolic authority" in terms of applicability of words as Word—*Verbum Dei*. He therefore teaches, not only for the local congregation but for the region, the generic church—all places and all times. I accept Scripture as authoritative in the literal (immediate and common) sense. Though I accept critical study—searching for truth from wherever it comes, Scripture mediates its own meaning and power—its authenticity is self-evident.

By occasional reference to Calvin, I dip into the Reformation movement, not only by way of the faith heritage in which I stand but in the tradition that Jean Calvin—a preacher, theologian—belonged. In Calvin's day, as in the early church and the patristics period preaching, Bible reading and commentary writing flourished. Thousands of sermons and commentaries abounded. It was also a time when adhering to Scripture, as in the Barmen Declaration in the era of Nazism, was considered "status confessions"—urgent, emergency orders of creedal moment. The faith itself was at stake.

The renowned Reformation historian Arthur Cochrane (*Reformed Confessions of the Sixteenth Century*, Louisville, KY: Westminister John Knox, 2003), finds in 1 Corinthians an expression of the primal credo of the earliest Christian community. The great epistle arises at a moment when life and death and the faith itself hang in the balance. Consider 11:23–26 and 15:3–7 as "capsule creeds."

> For I received of the Lord that which I also delivered unto you, that the Lord Jesus the same night in which he was betrayed took bread: and when he had given thanks, he brake it, and said Take eat: this is my body, which is broken for you: this do in remembrance of me. After the same manner also he took the cup, when he had supped, saying, this cup is the new testament in my blood: this do ye as oft as you drink it, in remembrance of me. For as often as ye eat this bread, and drink this cup, ye do show forth his death till he come. (1 Corinthians 11: 23–26 KJV)

The formulaic pattern—Rabbinic rhetoric—*paralambanein* (received) and *paradidonai* (delivered) is the same in 15:3–7:

> For I delivered unto you first of all that which I also received, how that Christ died for our sins according to the scriptures; And that he was buried, and that he rose again the third day according to the scriptures: and that he was seen of Cephas, the twelve, and last of all of me also . . .

We confront here a charter of life and death concerning God in Christ, deliverance from sin and death, assurance of resurrection and new life, the Eucharistic meal and saving-purposive companionship of Holy Spirit amid persecution and martyrdom, life and death, crisis and renewal, within and beyond this world and out into the future is the theological substance of this epistle. It is about God and humanity in this world. A profound treatise, it concerns the world beset by judgment and graced by salvation.

Paul preaches and addresses correspondence to a people who are yearning for contact with the living God. They search for a winsome way of life. They need saving righteousness—faith and life. In Calvin's day, as today, people want direct speech from and with God. They want access to the God-Word in their own vernacular language. They want Scripture in hand. They want vibrant and compelling faith and life for the living of such days. But do they—really?

Why then do they consort with idols and flirt with immoralities and injustices? They have been taught by the "apostle" who knew Torah by heart and preached and wrote in the tradition of prophetic elaboration of this "Way" of God. They also know that fellowship with God and with each other requires "holiness," which is righteousness. Despite this awareness they want their own tailor-made, domesticated creed and custom. They can't shed the residue of the old pagan ways. "I belong to Paul, to Apollos, to Christ"—not to the one God—the triune unity who alone is real, alive and efficacious, full of *exousia* and sovereign power. Now everything is at stake. A new realm, a kingdom, at the same time old and eternal, is at hand. All "new being is now 'en Christou'"—therefore repent, receive, and live anew.

This book is therefore written for my own congregation in Evanston—the church of an early (1954) Conference of the Ecumenical movement in the World Council of Churches. It contains very local preaching and teaching, commentary and reflection—offered in the hope of finding worthiness and usefulness in broader circles of church, religion, and society.

Theology—my discipline—according to Karl Barth is a work of the church. Even in his epitome position of the German academy and the preeminent theologian of the modern world—equal in stature to Augustine, Aquinas, and Calvin—his gospel, he said, was simply, "Jesus Loves me, this I know, for the Bible tells me so." The cardinal disciplines of the Kirchliche Dogmatik are therefore exegesis, dogmatics, and homiletics—written word, living word, and preached word. I trust that my first teacher of theology would approve of this effort of a *doktoran* and *nachfolger* to study the great concourse of "what God is now doing in the world" through a fine-grained analysis of the life of a local congregation—it's preaching, teaching, and community living.

So, 1 Corinthians and this congregation—here we go.

I. A DIVISIVE BODY IN A FRACTURED WORLD

In our analysis of this salient letter and the meaning it takes from and brings to Corinth and our congregation, we will want to address the parameters of truth pertaining to (1) the reality of God in Christ, (2) the situation in Corinth and today's world, and (3) our own congregation, including the broader church.

I begin this chapter by declaring my own persuasion in exegesis and exposition that embraces the biblical (God)—issues alongside those expressed in the commentaries by Augustine, Aquinas, Calvin, Will Orr and James Walther (*Anchor Yale Bible Commentaries*, New Haven, CT: Yale University Press, 1976), and Ken Bailey (from his post of church leadership in Palestine, Israel, and the Middle East, *Paul Through Mediterranean Eyes*, Downers Grove, IL: InterVarsity Press, 2011). I have also sought to familiarize myself in a surface way with the hundreds of commentaries in myriad tongues across history on this salient epistle to church and world.

My own perspectives grow out of my own theological diary that has focused in recent years on (1) interfaith work; (2) Middle East event interpretation, which in my reading all centers in the Palestine/Israel quandary that is the eye of the hurricane about terrorism; and (3) the underlying question of "what God is doing in this world—now."

The news during recent weeks has focused on the biblical land of Syria where the leadership dynasty of this fascinating interfaith land of Muslims and Orthodox Christians, along with a small "evangelical" presence, has for nearly one year met the uprising—Arab spring, peaceful protest—with brutal, suppressive killing of thousands of citizens provoking the protest of most nations of the world until Russia and China recently vetoed a UN resolution of censure and "crimes against humanity."

The "Free Syria" resistance movement, which now is receiving weapons as she fights the Assad rockets, army, and security forces, is Islamist in persuasion, mainly in the hands of Sunni Muslims. The Syrians I know are Christians who support the state, though they are deeply agonized by the killing of innocent civilians. They fear the fragile interfaith-tolerant nation will soon disappear. Ironically, the Assad government's few friends are the Shiah centers of power, such as Iran, which would pave the way for an even more Shariah state.

World (ecumenical) history is coming to focus today as never before in the Middle East. Though world powers fail to see this and focus their attention on Europe, the global economy, the United States, and Asia, the God-story, which is the determinative story of all others—economic, political, and theological—is unfolding in Israel/Palestine and environs.

Muslims now believe that Jews and Christians (especially Americans) are not to be trusted and they now wish to be free from the Western, propped up, "strong-men" regimes. In Iraq and Afghanistan, Christians have been expelled and Jews are suspect because of their Zionist loyalties. Egypt has dramatically cleansed its land of Jews where once hundreds of synagogues flourished. Coptic Christians have recently fallen under the attack of the Islamist majorities even though they and the evangelical community—Presbyterian Seminary and American University in Cairo—supported them in the Tahrir Square uprising and the eventual overthrow of the Mubarak regime.

This emergence of a new society in the Mediterranean and near-eastern world is replete with hope since the world depends so much on her material and spiritual resources. It also sends shudders of fear and trembling into the world because of the apocalyptic tenor of these developments. The body-politic of the world is either becoming fulsome or fractured—exactly Paul's vision in his warning and wish to Corinth.

Aside from the great block of neutrality in Russia, China, Asia, and Africa, the world in its spiritual/ethical foundation is fracturing today into two camps: "Eurabia" and "Judaeo-America." Europe is allied, via its incorporation of Eastern Europe, Turkey, and Western Asia, into a center of residual, nominal Christian and vibrant Islamic culture—the Crusades have come home to roost and we are not sure whether Jews are welcome. At the same time, America is the only fast and faithful friend of Israel and the epicenter of an Abrahamic interfaith world because of its vital Jewish and Islamic presence and conviction.

At the moment Iran, Korea, and to some extent the powerful Israel and Pakistan, are unpredictable threats to world peace.

In light of this historical and contemporary context, let us see the way Calvin overviews the opening chapter of 1 Corinthians:

In verse 8 Paul is preparing this cosmopolitan people for the dawning of a new day—the day "of the Lord." To this eschatology of history, Calvin also senses that a new spiritual horizon is rising for the world in the evangelical (*evangelisch*) awakening at this culminating moment in Axis-Time history—when Christianity and Islam are leading the world toward a new destiny—as the children of Israel whose history has been rendered universal by the God of Creation and incarnation.

In verse 10, Paul pleads that the congregation "be joined in one mind," be united in one "judgment" (*sententia/katartidzesthai*). Here Calvin follows the translation of Erasmus, adding the emphasis that the community be "knitted together—fitted and adjusted," mended from what has been fractured. As Calvin understood so well, the Hellenic and Hebraic—Greek and Jew—two Axis religions thought to be irreparably severed were being blended into one new Messianic/Sophic (wisdom) culture by Mesha/Christos—the God/Man who had appeared in Jesus of Nazareth. What happens here is profoundly deeper than something existential or parochial; it is cosmic and transcendent, a new beginning given the world.

II. WISE ENOUGH TO BE SO SMART? CHAPTER 1; AND III. MILK AND MEAT: HOLY FOOLS IN THE DIVINE NURSERY AND CRADLE OF THE WORLD, CHAPTER 2

We drove in at dusk to the small French town of Selestat, the old tenth-century Romanesque cathedral city exuded a golden tone and the shadowy interior of the church allowed only dim color to radiate from the sublime glass in the fading evening. We couldn't see the old priest and the young catechumen sitting in the front pew until we drew near and heard the faint sound of a simple hymn from the two voices: "*Il est né, le divin enfant*" (he is born, the divine infant). The priest was asking the young boy about his tender faith in this child-savior who appeared "in the deep mid-winter"—as Europe would have it—in Bethlehem of old.

Paul is waxing in such memories as he crafts his epistle, perhaps on the shores of Asia Minor in Ephesus, to his beloved community just across the Aegean Sea (as the raven flies) in Corinth. "As babes in Christ I nursed you with milk until you were ready for meat" (1 Cor 3:2). Calvin's thought and commentary is steeped in the nativity theology of the divine infant. In his commentary on 1 Corinthians, Calvin writes that Paul came to his fragile flock "as babes in Christ"—"*comme enfants en Christ*" (3:1). He goes on to say that the nascent body of Christ in Corinth is "torn into pieces"—"*par pieces et morceaux.*"

This section of the epistle is quite amazing. The kindergarten kids are a divisive lot. Their squabbles threaten their own authentic nourishment with the milk of life. They also impede the sharing of the gospel grace of life with others. Yet their infancy in faith is the very assurance of their strength and growth. When Berlioz composed "L'enfance du Christ," he suggested in melody and mood that the strong meat imparted by the child born to die is mediated only as we are prepared to "become as little children" while we nourish one another with the "bread" (milk of life).

In his insightful study of the early Christian community, Rodney Stark claims that the power to survive and endure, to suffer and grow can best be attributed to the "nursing" commitment of the early church. The infants and the sick, the old and the deformed, the poor and the derelict were honored rather than done in or put away. In plague, the healers remained near. The dying were shepherded home. As Paul wrote earlier in this epistle (1:27), "God chose the foolish, poor and weak things of the world to confound the wise and great" (my conflation). Actually, childlike collaboration is the secret of successful mission: "I planted, Apollo watered, but God gave the increase" (3:6).

Pastor Ray dealt with the movement and structure of this section of the epistle with his customary skill as Bible-exegete, theologian, and pastor. He began by remembering when he was in Bible college in Fort Wayne, Indiana, and his wife, Judith, delivered their firstborn girl. Anxious and sleep-weary parents, they wanted the newborn to grow up fast—to feed and change herself and to sleep solidly like a teenager. It didn't happen. As with Paul and his infant congregation in Corinth, meat could only follow milk later—much later.

PORNEIA AND PASSOVER: CAN IMPURITY BE A PUBLIC SIN? CHAPTERS 3 AND 4

Pastor Ray then interpreted verses 1–3 on the tension of living carnally or spiritually by reflecting on our own drag down into the flesh, absorbed in ill will, depression, anger, and party spirit, commending rather quiet trust in the Holy Spirit of God who conveyed peace and composure.

He then elucidated his thesis that the pericope reflected the substance of the entire letter as God's temple—that the Kingdom was mediated with specificity into the world by the offered, resurrected, and ever-living body of Christ (what the book of Hebrews sees as the new temple) which, in turn, was constituted by our bodies, temples entrusted into our stewardship—living sacrifices—as the eyes, arms, hands, ears, and so forth of the body of Christ in the world. The realm of kingdom, he concluded, was this concentric circle configuration of the interpenetrating body: "You are Christ's and Christ is God's" (3:22, 23).

In three practical points, he elaborated the chapter: (1) emotional maturity grounds spiritual maturity; (2) healthy relationships between leaders and people are called for; and (3) all accede to the supervening kingdom (body) of God. In "that day"—the culminating and final "audit" day, all human work will be tested by fire.

A theme I found running through the Scripture, song ("my hope is built on nothing less than Jesus' blood and righteousness"; "lead on, O King eternal—not with swords, or drums but deeds") and sermon was the thread of covenant. Kingdom is a phenomenon of belief (participatory piety) and action ("through deeds of love and mercy, the heavenly Kingdom comes"). Salvation and service go hand in hand in biblical religion. Saving grace is a matter of being delivered from sin and death and of enacting social justice. Notice the decalogical structure of the book—quarrelling, fornication, strife, idolatry, arrogance—is a dead giveaway.

A summarial passage of Calvin captures that preacher-reformer's persuasion on this chapter:

> I have planted, Apollos watered. [Paul] unfolds more clearly the nature of that ministry by a similitude, in which the nature of the word and the use of preaching are most appropriately depicted. That the earth may bring forth fruit, there is need of plowing and sowing, and other means of culture; but after all this has been carefully done, the husbandman's labor would be of no avail, did not the Lord from heaven give the increase, by the breaking forth of the sun, and still more by his wonderful and secret influence ... Ministers are as it were husbandmen, that plow and sow. Then follow other helps, for example, irrigation ...
>
> —"First Epistle to the Corinthians," in Calvin's *Commentary on Corinthians*, Grand Rapids, MI: Baker, p.127

Calvin exquisitely intertwines the natural and supernatural in the flourishing of kingdom. We cannot do it without God and God chooses not to do it without us—as we offer careful stewardship, faithful preaching, and persistent cultivation (*"continue et soit touiours entretenue"*).

Chapter 4 draws to conclusion this part of the letter. It is one of the most powerful texts in early Christian literature—vying with chapters 13 and 15 in this great epistle for honored position in this sacred Scripture. Here we find Paul—the undisputed author—the ironic philosopher, admonishing prophet, and nurturing pastor. This composition, along with Romans, may therefore be for pastors a favorite section of Pauline Scripture.

The passage then invites contemporary paraphrase which I here offer:

"Where do you come off being of 'another kingdom [NEB],' so far above everyone else? You are so satisfied, so rich; you have become kings. We're sorry we were away for the coronation.

"We, on the other hand, were given up for dead—a spectacle to heaven and earth. We are fools and you are so smart; we are weaklings—you gladiators; you are revered, we are homeless beggars; we are famished and thirsty, naked, kicked around—not even a cardboard box on the street for a bed; being cursed we bless in return; reviled we don't strike back; our character assassinated, we hold back our fury; we are the world's trash, the refuse of the garbage dumps."

Besides repudiating the gospel invitation to all great and small, and polarizing the grand equality of the divine economy, the drawn disparity portrays to the world an elitism and the ascendency of a ruling class that is the very antithesis of the good news of the "law of Christ."

In this same mood, 2 Corinthians 8 uses the image of the manna in the wilderness (Exod 16:15). In this daily provision, God freely spreads with the "breaking morning," the "recreation of the new day." Surplus and abundance—daily bread—sufficient to the day on one condition: that it is not greedily hoarded and stashed away by hoarding but rather shared and distributed.

In this commentary, Calvin seizes not only instruction of the universal availability and equality of members of the body of Christ but also the formation of material equity among the whole human family. He wrote in his economic writings of the "mystery of the rich and the poor" where each gifts the other. "God will that there be equality among us. That means that none should have too much and none too little" (2 Cor 8:15). This passage, along with the writing of the prophets, would inspire Karl Marx in his early political-economic writings three hundred years later.

Ironically, it was the Calvinist movement in the Rhineland, Britain, and Scotland and America that would fuel the capitalist upsurge and concentration of wealth, including the polarizations of rich and poor in the contemporary world. Catholic, Pentecostal, and Islamic pieties display greater attention to the poor in today's fractured globe.

In America, the epitome of Max Weber's "capitalist universe," we now witness the infamous 1 percent (75 percent of whom are doctors, lawyers, and businessmen) harping out of the lap of luxury that "we can't worry about the very poor; they have their safety nets"—frayed as they are. It sounds eerily like Charles Dickens' celebrated banker, Ebenezer

Scrooge: "You have the poorhouses, the alms houses, and the debtors' prisons." The filthy rich have lost the sanctifying and redeeming power of biblical wisdom, which knows that all we possess is "filthy rags"—a Pauline turn of phrase—and that wealth is indeed Calvin's test of accountability: to share that equality may prevail among us, i.e., none should have too much and none too little. How desperately today we need to remind the Warren Buffetts, Bill Gateses, Mitt Romneys, and Mark Zuckermans that the greater the fortune they amass, the greater is *God's* expectation when they face the inevitable penultimate and ultimate accounting.

Pastor Erica addressed chapter 4 in this way:

It was her first sermon as associate pastor. With her worship coordinator and music team, she had crafted a moving Eucharistic liturgy in the mode of Taize—so reminiscent of the early Passover Paschal in the Jesus, early resurrection, and Pauline communities when Christians and Jews made observance together. Observance at synagogues such as Dura-Europos, Capernaum, and (Upper Room) Western Gate in Jerusalem involved baptism and chatechesis, scriptural reading, prophetic interpretation (preaching), supper/eucharist (Passover), and proselytic, evangelistic sending was captured in this service.

We sang two hymns with paschal (Lamb of God) themes. First, a praise song:

"You are the God of the broken, the friend of the weak

"You are the God of the humble. You are the humble King"

... And then the ancient Mass hymn, Agnus Dei:

"Lamb of God, thou takest away the sin of the world, have mercy on us."

In her communion meditation, she walked through the major sections of chapter 4, unfolding her thesis about "Honest to God leadership."

Transparent leadership means leading from and through to God, not to our own image. In Corinth, such diversions and impediments were always getting in the way.

Whether we lead or follow in particular instances (our child-homilist reminds us that we all assume both roles), we always defer or become a mediator of the one leader's leading—Jesus as true human and true God.

Pastor Erica brought the message home with examples from her own experience.

For myself, the distortion Pastor Erica reported has come from the supervening desire for erudition and eloquence (1 Cor 1 and 2), the professor/pastor's occupational hazard rather than being content to be a channel for God and truth–the vocation of both preacher and teacher.

That week was also the annual Washington Prayer Breakfast which was addressed by President Obama. The events of that day were hauntingly resonant with the concerns of 1 Corinthians:

> This [importance of prayer] is no different today for millions of Americans, and it's certainly not for me. I wake up each morning and I say a brief prayer, and I spend a little time in Scripture and devotion. And from time to time, friends of mine, some of who are here today, friends like Joel Hunter or T. D. Jakes, will come by the Oval Office or they'll call on the phone or they'll send me a e-mail, and we'll pray together, and they'll pray for me and my family, and for our country.

President Obama said his policy arguments stem from his interpretation of his Christian faith. For the wealthy to give up tax breaks, he says, is simply following the scriptural mandate: "To whom much is given, much shall be required."

Whitney Houston was found dead today (Feb. 11, 2012) in her hotel room in Los Angeles near the scene for the Grammy awards, at which she was to attend (evidence was that her death was not intentional). The words from her most famous song still echo through our minds and hearts, "and I'll . . . always love you." "Her demons," said one friend, "finally brought her down." At her memorial service a few days later, her good friend Kevin Costner reflected: "Whitney asked, was I good enough? Was I pretty enough? . . . This, in the end, was what brought her down."

Whitney knew from her church and Bible background (Aretha Franklin was her godmother) that her demons were within herself and within the world around her. They were in the hounding paparazzi (now everyone with a cell phone) that would never leave her alone until they drove her into the ground—like Princess Diana under the Paris overpass; they were in the screaming adulation of her millions of devotees and in the snares of extraordinary wealth and popularity. Danger lies in fame; her demons were in the drug scene—omnipresent all around us—insidiously destructive when joined with alcohol addiction—waiting to pounce—to sow discord and devastation; the demons were in our laissez faire neglect—unwilling to admonish in love even those whom we love.

In chapter 5 of 1 Corinthians, Paul is pondering this frightful enigma. And beginning with the profound probe and human and communal freedom, good—that is God—and evil, and onto the sublime hymn of love in chapter 13. He sings with Whitney the song of agape—divine-human love—eternal within and without, "and I'll . . . always love you."

The biblical cosmology speaks of *demonoi* and *diaboloi*—those forces which tear us apart and sever us from God, self, and the other. These are at enmity with the *symboli*—the healing, bringing-together impulses of the Holy Spirit and the one God whom for the church is in Christ.

The concepts of unity and solidarity are hard to understand in our age that is so excessive about individuality and "do your own private thing." Corinth and Calvin understood the solidarity of the body. It is reported that there is immorality (*porneia*) among you (5:1). Not only was there the equivalent of private Internet porn on your own tablet or cell phone But open promiscuity was out in the community, and the omnipresent "behavior police" reported it. These reports travelled the land and sea miles to Paul. Someone in the body did it and someone turned "him" in. In Mishnah—the manual of Hebraic case-law—stoning was prescribed for having "sexual relations" with one's mother, his father's wife, his daughter-in-law, a male, or a beast. As far as we know, this punishment was seldom used—though we find hints of stoning threat in the New Testament and in contemporary Mullah and mob-induced Shariah law (Sannhedrin 7: 4). Here, someone was cohabiting with his father's wife. In an ironic twist and inconsistency in the tradition, infidelity and male sex-philandering was often overlooked in the Jewish sexual ethic. Even today, when fidelity and marriage seems to be disappearing—at least from the world of America—this breach was unconscionable, deserving of what seems to be punishment too harsh for Jesus: "leave him to Satan for the destruction of the flesh" (5:5).

Calvin asks, "Why ought they have mourned over another person's sin?" He writes, "In consequence of the communion that exists among the members of the Church, it was becoming that all should feel hurt at so deadly a fall on the part of one of their number." Beyond that he continues, "the whole society is in a manner polluted" (*Commentary*, 5:1, 2). He recalls how the whole nation of Israel brought on the "wrath of God" by the sacrilege of one man—Achan (Josh 7:1).

Bailey makes clear how the Semitic languages and rhetoric (Hebraic, Aramaic—Jesus' tongue) and Arabic, which is the mutation of Jewish

Christianity, frames such a situation. In such an experience, one body is organically conjoined to the collective (corporate) body and even the divine "being of God" (ontological and deontological) itself was intricated and defamed. In the Emmanuel body—the "God with us" or Messiah body of Christ—Godself is drawn into the mud. By virtue of creation and incarnation, each and every body is caught up in the righteous act or unrighteous breach (incorporation). Your body is temple—you were bought with a price. Selling out the body—e.g., slavery—is ironically intensified by such divine purpose. As one low-level employee once wisely remarked, "God don't make no trash."

Now Calvin is clear to affirm that guilt (and grace/freedom) is personal, and one who is innocent cannot and will not be condemned by God for guilt by association. But we are encouraged by God to observe the common good and keep individual bodies and the corporate body pure and holy so as to enhance the inner morale and outer credibility of the faith community.

We remember that the new Christian constituency of the Corinthian Church was made up of wrong-doers who had repented and renewed by the grace of God. These persons of tender conscience should not be misled by behavioral hypocrisy by the "role models" in the community. Also, the youth of tender conscience should be encouraged in the Torah—"law of Christ," way of life and admonished against idolatry, immorality and injustice—the rightful stewardship of body and mind.

Today those rigorous ethics, once painfully enforced in Puritan-derived societies like ours, are too often shown by our leaders—parents; church leaders; neighbors; political, business, and entertainment figures—to have been exchanged by an ethic touting, "it's only wrong if you get caught." So one must ask the question of whether the "purity" ethic of the religious community can ever be applied to the general secular public and how such a behavioral code might be inculcated and enforced.

A different light on this issue of banishment is shed by Ken Bailey's thoughtful commentary. With his extraordinary knowledge of the influence of Middle Eastern perspectives on New Testament materials, Bailey sees 1 Cor 5:1–13 belonging to a larger unit beginning in chapter 4, and related to other materials involving Paul's absence and the dispatch of Timothy. Bottom line, Who am I to Judge? Paul writes, in effect, take care of this matter internally in the church. Send him out—shun him, exclude him from communion—this way he may be saved in the end.

Bailey's instruction is part of a broader Semitic (Jewish and Muslim?) wisdom with which he is most familiar among Bible scholars. In sum, it cries out—Get your act together. Don't blame God for bad things and don't expect God to take "care of things" if you refuse to care yourselves. In sharp admonishing speech, Paul speaks sternly to the church . . . I'm away now; take care of the church yourselves. I'm with you always—as is Christ our Lord and His paraclete strengthener—but you have to take care of these matters yourself. What else is the church—the local congregation, even the larger community—if it is not to build up and keep strong God's own people committed to our care?

Pastor Ray works the notion in this way:

> Paul followed up with these words: "For I wrote to you out of much affliction and anguish of heart and with many tears, not to cause you pain but to let you know the abundant love that I have for you." (2 Cor 2:4)

> And then he said, "For such a one, this punishment by the majority is enough, so you should rather turn to forgive and comfort him, or he may be overwhelmed by excessive sorrow. So I beg you to reaffirm your love for him." (2 Cor 2:6–8)

So it appears that the church's stand against this sinful practice was painful for Paul and the congregation; it was both loving and effective. It forced the man and the woman to reexamine their ways, return to the Lord and now he tells them to open their arms, their hearts, and welcome them home, forgive them.

Mourning indicates deep love and regard. Creative admonition is not "giving the fallen the boot." It is holding out the hands of repentance, return, and redemption.

Take a current case study: President Obama has directed the national, state, and city departments of health to guarantee the provision of "reproductive health" services—including the legal and ethical service of contraception for women, even poor women—through publically funded health insurance. Churches are exempted to honor Roman Catholic and "Evangelical" conscience on this matter. The rub comes with hospitals, universities, and other public institutions related to the church that seek to provide this service to non-Catholic employees and even the 50-plus percent of Roman Catholic employees who do not share the churches' contraceptive ethic. Put in Calvin and Paul in Corinth's moral rhetoric, how can the purity ethic be coerced on nonadherents of the underlying faith? Early Christian sex-ethics is derived from Judaism (resistance to Roman paganism) ethics. That religious ethos, shared with Jews and then Muslims (Jewish Christians?), found three snares out there in the extra-religious world: idolatry, impurity, and money. These powers—often societal virtues—were seen as treacherous temptations. Often the lures were called the world, the flesh, and the devil. So where and how does the Christian relational ethic take public form, except in the banal money pitch, "find God's match for you"—advertisements and online dating?

Of greater relevance today from this theme in Pauline Christian (and public) instruction are three highly damaging crimes and sins: Sex-slavery, sex-subjugation, and salacious sexuality. All of these practices are rendered illicit by Paul's exposition of the underlying sex-marriage commandment breach that falls under the rubric of porneia (fornication).

Sex-slavery is defined as having one's freedom seized by another person, group, corporation, or nation as one's body is sold for the abuse by others. Historically, nations like Japan and Germany, and modern societies like Cambodia, Thailand, the United States, and Eastern Europe have been havens for adult sex trafficking as well as the more grievous New Testament sin, *arsenokoitai*, (child exploitation and abuse), including child prostitution, child pornography, and child-sex tourism. We often wrongly associate this pederasty with what is called homophilia and homosexuality, which may be consensual, genuinely loving, and not a violation of one's neighbor. The sin/crime is particularly troubling in America, the citadel of freedom, purism and Puritanism, and business. The way this ends up is simple: the business of America is business and that business can even be guns or sex.

Sex-subjugation is a more critical and controversial matter. We're not sure what to do in personal, parochial, and public ethics with patriarchal communities—Amish, Mormon, orthodox Jews and Muslims, and evangelical Christians. Even Chinese and Korean families—with wife and children trailing *pater familias*—irritate our equality sensibilities. When Taliban ban women from schools and abused wives in Afghanistan immolate themselves or expose children to death in the frigid cold—something has gone terribly wrong. Poverty or profound wealth, disparity of rich and poor, is often associated with neglect and abuse of women and children. In all spiritual and ethical wisdom, the well-being of these vulnerables is the index of the justice and righteousness of a people.

One issue must be made clear: from the biblical foundations of Torah, the religious corruptions of idolatry and immorality (in Baalism, for example, through the purity accents of apocalyptic and ultimately orthodox Christianity, resisting Graeco-Roman indulgence and then Islam's reform of Judao-Christian and Pagan immorality and promiscuity) fundamentalism and Puritanism is a reaction against failing and false faith. Salacious sexuality or indulgent promiscuity prompts the pious to cry out, "search me, o Lord and try me . . ." Our reactive religiously fanatic culture and the dominant pleasure-oriented, free-love culture from which it demurs—indeed is repelled—are siblings of the same parents. Righteousness will only be revived by holistic faith—personal, congregational, national, and global.

My evidence is from over fifty years work as a teaching and consulting bioethicist. On birth ethics (one segment of sexuality ethics), research shows that good maternal health provision and availability of the subsequent spectrum of sustaining ministries of women's, maternal, and child health is now diminishing the worldwide incidence of abortion.

Here is my case: On the perplexing case just stated, contraception (which is now part of a spectrum of life and health enhancing procedures: celibacy and prevention technique, birth control by myriad means, morning-after intervention [RU486], early-term abortion, and even the new possibility of genetic activation of pluripotent eggs) is good policy, though heart-wrenching and morally ambiguous. Such life decisions should be undertaken carefully, conscientiously—in accord with Godly and scriptural ethics, as well as in accord with the finest rational and secular knowledge and wisdom.

This means that we must honor nascent and present lives (even revering the sacred value of potential lives, e.g., embryos). We should aid girls and women to safeguard their sexual and reproductive health, and encourage boys and men toward sexual responsibility. We should resist public and parochial institutions when they seek to coerce persons either on the presence or absence of the aforementioned preventive and interventive measures. We should uphold one another in love and care. At the end of the day, we must especially embrace the (and the world's) women and children in our families, congregations, and societies.

1 Corinthians 6:12-20, Calvin's Take

Calvin, in his *Commentary on Corinthians*, begins his discussion of chapter 6 of the letter with these words:

> It is probable that the Corinthians, even up to that time (the time of the Epistle) retained much of their former licentiousness (Fr. *licence*) and had still the savour of the morals in their city . . . when vices stalk abroad with impunity custom is regarded as law.

An astounding and extraordinary claim. Calvin considers Paul through the eyes of sixteenth-century Paris, Strasbourg, and Geneva. A fragile new theocracy, which will yield to the world democratic order, it displaces an old Roman theocracy. Both saw church-imposed moral order on the public order as a good and right thing. Conversely, Paul seems to think of Rome as an order-providing realm. Well and good, but dangerous when it claims its own ultimacy and divinity—demanding worship. For Paul, even the church-persecuting Empire is the provision of God, an authority deserving respect—until the church becomes empire. Calvin believes in the Corpus Christianum *seculorum* of Augustine and Aquinas as a holding force against the disintegration of civil order and the protector of the church.

Drawing on Paul and Corinth, Calvin has a different vision. The church is seen as leaven in a spoiled lump. She must clean up her act for the sake of her own constituency and to witness a clear message to the world. Calvin's political points are intriguing and his spiritual point is decisive for the integrity and preservation of church and world.

Calvin's bottom line is a demand on the church and a hope for the world. He feels that the Corinthians and the Swiss (and we might add for our part—the Chicagoans) saw prevalent injustice, impiety, and impurity not only as legal but as good and right—they called evil good and perhaps good—evil. He hopes that the public order—the civil magistrate—will come under the sway, perhaps even coercion and persuasion of the kingdom of God and decide to crack down on such immorality. If the society will not clean up its act, the church must live out sexual righteousness as a counter-cultural witness. She must keep her house in order. After all, she was bought with such a price.

The second thrust of Calvin's argument is that public and parochial corruption is caused by *"liaisons dangereux"*—false attachments. This sociological notion is undergirded by a theological anthropology—a view of the person. Calvin is blunt, strenuous, and full of warning. One is either joined to Christ and Holy Spirit (Who is Lord? 2 Cor 3:17). Therefore, each person is holy, or one belongs to the world and is profane. This costly identity choice is expressed at home, church, and world. The Amish see it starkly but correctly: We are in, but not of, the world. One joined to the world's way is profane, even though he may go through the motions of church. We become what we love.

Now—for me and today, I'm not sure I believe this body-mysticism where good or bad association defines our being and either lifts us up or takes us down. I tend to celebrate both secularity and spirituality. What is certain about Calvin's position is that we do indeed become what we believe. That to which we are joined becomes our life. Our ontological choices—choices of our being, being in God or in something else—are life or death decisions. We remember the great passage of Joshua 24: "I set before you life and death—choose life—as for me and my family, we will serve God." One question we are left with is that of presidential candidate Rick Santorum who posed this, Should persons of faith be allowed to express that voice in the public sphere or should persons of faith—whatever on earth that means—be excluded from that forum? Some theocrats even go further and say that they should have a voice that is privileged. Though I find Santorum's conviction that President Obama is a *snob* in his belief that all should have the possibility of going to college and that President Kennedy made him nauseous in his insistence that the separation of church and state was part of religious integrity to be a bit extreme, I agree with Santorum's plea that the faith voice be allowed back into the public square. This is the issue with which Paul, Calvin, Pastor Ray, and myself all struggle.

Here is one reason. Ambassador Jon Huntsman—a Latter-day Saint, faith brother of Romney—said recently that American society is now searching for what it believes. We must look now for the new "next big thing" for America. He's right! I would slightly alter that to say that we are called to envision what is the next big thing for God and his world. God is not as invested in "the exceptional nation" as we are.

Forgive me if I wax partisan and political for a moment. Such are the expectations and privileges of professors and Rush Limbaugh. I believe that faith belongs in the public sphere but not in the sense of the religious right or left. And religion does not hold the trump card—neither Shariah nor the religious right/law has the last word.

What is the next big thing for America, Huntsman asks? I ask further, is it human rights and human justice and a commitment to Kant's "perpetual peace" or is it libertarian freedom, free-enterprise economics, and Hobbe's Leviathan state of "permanent war"? Is it the common good state, with social security and public health provision or is it the laissez-faire state—no stimulus, handouts, or bailouts? Is it the lean and mean state where programs like education and care for the poor and old are relegated to the states—where New York and California thrive and Alabama, Mississippi, and Texas starve—though capital punishment, incarceration of minorities, and suppression of immigrants remain alive and well?

And what view and person will become the national voice? Will it be the Pennsylvania Catholic mime, the Michigan "born again" Mormon buy-outer, or perhaps the "all things to all men"—"when in Rome do as the Romans do"—or even the Franklin Graham-certified Christian lad from Illinois?

So, in conclusion of this scriptural pericope of 1 Corinthians 6, we turn to four heartland mainline Presbyterians named William Orr, James Walther, Ken Bailey, and Ken Vaux—all who hail from the epicenter of world Calvinism, which is a hundred mile radius circle around Pittsburgh. Most pundits and political demographers believe that the 2012 elections will be decided in this geographical circle—Eastern Ohio and Western Pennsylvania.

Pastor Ray and I are part of that "lesser Mafia" and though not a graduate there, I've come to respect the great center of thought which is the oldest Presbyterian Seminary in America. Professor Bob Kelly, John Gerstner, and Pastor Keith Brown, for whom our first son, Keith, was named, were products of the church I served in Mt. Lebanon.

Orr and Walther, in *Anchor Bible I*, show that in verse 12, Paul uses the verb *sympherei* (symphony) for what the church is meant to be. Not cacophony or a raucous brass or tinkling cymbal—remember 1 Corinthians 13—but everyone working together in harmony, every instrument contributing its part, creating beautiful music. Unrighteous, discordant people, the commentators write, do not inherit the kingdom. Beginning in verse 9, we find four areas of disqualifying injustices—modes of unrighteousness: sex sins, property sins, sins that destroy the mind, and sins that destroy the neighbor.

Orr and Walther continue: When one joins to a prostitute he (she) becomes one flesh with the partner. This occurs with casual sex, promiscuous sex, sex slavery or sex trafficking, no matter how impersonal and detached we think these to be. As we saw in the last chapter of this book, one becomes intricate, implicated, conjoined with that somebody, and this is much more involved than the act of conception. The basic teaching is that we should not defile our body or that of another—both of which are temples of God. We can't sell out or buy out because we were each bought with such a price. Promiscuous heterosexuality or homosexuality is not to be condoned in the church or civic community.

We're back in nineteenth-century Evanston with no drugs—especially booze or cigarettes—and avoid the pimps, stalking guys, or loose women. Keep this soil-sport south of Howard Street. Don't come near Frances Willard's home (founder of the Women's Christian Temperance Union), Garrett Seminary, the Women's Bible Institute, or the Methodist, Baptist, or Presbyterian Churches. Mind your business and turn your energy to helping slaves escape along the "underground railroad."

Ken Bailey is from the New Wilmington Missionary Conference on the campus of Westminster College. I worked here when I was a young minister in Mt. Lebanon and Pastor Ray was the preacher there last summer and the students and families of our congregation were there as usual. Bailey is a mainline Presbyterian, as we are all of us sharing a commitment to bodily chastity and a deep and abiding sense of mercy to those who stumble as we seek to be a church of mercy and diversity in the parish and community.

With the eyes of one who has lived for forty years in the Middle East, Bailey understands the Semitic senses of human solidarity and scriptural holiness. Children of Abraham do not burn Bibles, Torah scrolls, or the Quran. In our chapter, you will note an interesting joining of the first five commandments—which now are all sexual—comparable to apostasy, idolatry, defamation of sacred place (Sabbath), and parental/familial obligation. The God Commandments are woven into the interhuman commandments. Indicative, God has done, demands imperative; therefore, you must! Paul, you remember, believes in the validity of the three covenants—with Isaac, Ishmael, and Christ. Bailey, more than any other commentator, understands this Middle Eastern–Semitic crucible of the three faiths of Abraham.

V. LOVE AND LAW: MARRIAGE AND BODY, CHAPTER 5

Pastor Ray talked of our propensity to "marinate in our anger" when we have had a fallout with a fellow parishioner or neighbor. We threaten to walk out, to gossip profusely, spilling our anger onto everyone in sight, stewing in the juices of bitterness. Beyond his clergy credentials, "the Jamaican" is obviously a seaside chef.

Today, we'd rather go to law with our disputes. We have created a law apparatus (establishment) that, in America, has roughly seven times the lawyers per capita than any other nation in the world. Of the celebrated 1 percent who own the 99 percent of our national wealth, 85 percent are doctors, businessmen or—you guessed it—lawyers. There is corporate law and domestic law, medical law and educational law, divorce law and child law—and on and on. The profession has successfully cordoned off almost all realms of human life—personal, family, community, state, national, and international. It has made itself the arbiter through whom all issues must pass. Some nations designate domestic and family law—sexuality, marriage and divorce, inheritance, death and dying—to the church, rabbinic, Canon or Shariah law, further complicating the matter.

Paul's counsel is that persons first deal personally with each other in matters of Torah law, law of Christ, or moral law. Seek out the wise counselors of the congregation (think of Moses mediating disputes at the public gate in Numbers 11). Share the issue with them and heed their judgment. Don't stomp out in rage, refuse to talk forever and ever or "resort to law." Persist in search of confession, apology, forgiveness, and reconciliation (even in cases of rape and murder in some places in Africa—cf. truth and reconciliation commissions). After hearing this sermon, I held up the example I once heard in a sermon. An African gentleman had a knockdown, drag-out dispute with his neighbor, of which both resolved to take to their grave. One gave in and pitched a tent in the neighbor's front yard, saying he wouldn't leave until peace came. He lived there three months, and one day the other man came out—with a cup of tea.

How does Calvin address the issues raised in the second part of 1 Corinthians 6 (vs. 9–20)—matters about "God and the body"? First, he places the issues in the matrix of Paul's memorized Torah—the Decalogue. This Scripture—which was also the substance of the prophets—we recall—was conceived in Paul's day as pure Verbum Dei. This was the singular moment when God not only spoke, but actually wrote it down.

Paul says in my Bible translation: "you are all aware that only persons 'made right' [with God and humanity] will receive the Kingdom from God." Not pornophiles, idol-lovers, those unfaithful to their partner, child molesters, inverts (self-absorbed), robbers, enviers, those out of control with intoxications, those angry and consumed with bitterness, and those who extort others (*arpages*)—there is no place in God's realm for these abusers of God, self, and others. These folk—though precious to God—are missing the mark of righteousness and kingdom—love of the neighbor in Godself.

Calvin here is his proto-puritan, legalistic, but also his blessedly humanistic self. God seeks reverence to his holiness; personal integrity (sometimes called purity), goodness, and care to others around you. God delights with persons who honor and protect the weak, who are pious, just—good stewards of the grace of life. Calvin still used the ancient construal of good and evil—temptation—the world, the flesh, and the devil in ancient imagery (a diabolical, that is, all torn up world, "with devils filled," in Luther's crude speech), powers ever threatening to bring us down. Such images are hard to decipher in real life and to make relevant to contemporary experience. You've been there, he concludes. This dangerous and destructive existence was the dissolute life from which the Christ-Spirit rescued you. You were down and almost out, but God in Christ pulled you from the collapsing building. He placed you on higher ground.

The following passage captures Calvin's message:

> That his [Paul's] threatening may have more weight, he says "be not deceived," by which expression he admonishes them not to flatter themselves with a vain hope, as persons are accustomed, by extenuating their offenses, to inure themselves to contempt of God. No allurements [poisons] are more dangerous than those which encourage us in our sins.
>
> —Ken Bailey, *Jesus Through Middle Eastern Eyes*, Downer's Grove, IL: InterVarsity, 2012

Rather than gathering the diffuse energies of our impulsive lives into an integrated (symbolic) whole we succumb to diabolic "tearing apart"—vice has been transfigured into virtue and we live the lie imagining that all is well.

The bodies of persons are parables of the social corporation and corporately signs (symbols) of the body of God. Our illusions that bodies are flesh-lumps to be kneaded as needed, amassed for evil purpose, manipulated, degraded and ignored, wounded and killed at will, numbers and statistics. That we own our bodies, possess them as they reside in our disposal, is dangerous dehumanization. Such depersonalization is not only abrogation of our stewardship of self and our shepherding of one another in the garden of the world; it is blasphemy against the body of Godself. Our bodies are sacred vessels and sacred trust—"We are not our own . . ."; "We are temples of the Holy Spirit"—"Therefore glorify God in your bodies." You were bought with a great price.

Calvin's foundational premise was that human lives whole and well, free and just—human lives fulfilled—were the glory of God.

First Corinthians 7: 1–40 (excluding vs.14–24, an awkward interlude as embarrassing as Paul's admonition that women shut up in the church, and of Luther's, that the fair sex remain ensconced in *Kirche, Küche, und mit den Kindern*), rather, addresses our uncertainty about whether we face a short time and end time or long time horizon: The horizon of bodies in the world.

We are still in Lent—the revelry of Fat Tuesday and the sobriety of Ash Wednesday remains through Lent 2, 3, 4 . . . It is like the prolonged season of ordinary time that will eventually be upon us. Pastor Erica will guide us through this passage that seeks to describe body stewardship whether one be single or married, gay or straight, whether we, and indeed the human race, are here for the long haul or face an imminent end.

We have mentioned in previous notes the sociological data in America, even in the Middle East (cf. Egypt), where less than 50 percent of eligible singles now choose to marry and have children, or are otherwise discouraged from permanent commitments because work is scarce and economic conditions are prohibitive.

In a perhaps related phenomenon the great sociobiologist Edward Wilson at Harvard who, in addition to his masterpiece, *Sociobiology*, wrote another significant book entitled *On Human Nature* (Cambridge, MA: Harvard University Press, 2004). In it he argues that homosexuality occurs in predictable ratios in humans and in all animal species depending on populational density and carrying capacity of the environment. He also contends that the proclivity of early human populations on earth to designate single, homophilic (non-reproductive and perhaps naturally or selectively sterile) persons to be shamans and priests was an adaptive evolutionary mechanism as well as a religious-ministerial adaptation. We may ask whether Paul's ruminations in this passage of his first letter to Corinth are related to this phenomenon.

My doctoral teacher, Helmut Thielicke, in his many biblical-theological works, e.g., *The Waiting Father* (Cambridge, UK: Lutterworth, 1987), always noted that all New Testament writers—even their predecessors in late apocalyptic Judaism—believed that final judgment and the end of time and the world was imminent. Paul also seemed to resonate with the counsel of his *Kyrios* Jesus that we were not given to know the times and places, hidden from even his Lordly cognizance, and that the parousia of the expected kingdom might very well be indefinitely or infinitely delayed. More common was the view that final consummation was believed by theology as well as science today as absolutely certain—maybe in a moment (*augenblick*—blinkling of the eye)—at the last trumpet (ref: 1 Cor 15). So in this lesson of Paul, we ponder Cullman's mystery of Christ and time.

My comments center on two issues: (1) commandments, call, and choice; and (2)marriage, mourning, and Maranatha. The text continues the gospel in miniature exploration of the entire letter: What is it to believe and act well—in person, in parish, and in public. Who is God? How is the one God of all creation shown and known in the face of Jesus Christ? How does Emmanuel—God and Spirit in the world—shape a way of life (belief and value) within the people of the world? In interfaith hermeneutics, I believe that the composite Scriptures of the Abrahamic faiths have become universal truth.

The first verses of this pericope have to do with how one is incorporated into the life-world of God as circumcision (or baptism from the Christian tradition), which bestows the name and spirit of identity, which the Spirit of God, the conveyor of Torah—the way of God life—has mediated into our own existence. Pentecost is Shavuot—the celebration of the receipt of God's way of faith and ethics into the community of belief and practice—God's elect people on earth. The mark of personal and communal belonging is engraved in the flesh and confirmed in fire, wind, and water—the symbols of Holy Spirit.

Paul here says that changing one's status, i.e., vocation, now is unnecessary since the time is short. Stay married or single, Jew or Greek, slave or free: remain ready and mobile for assignment. Be rooted in the word so that you always have the right confession for the time and circumstance at hand. Be all things to all people; know their languages and cultures—near Eastern and Indian, African and European, Aramaic/Arabic, Greek and Latin. Have the word in season by disciplined study, contemplation, and prayer. Address critically, prophetically, and practically people in their life-situations—sexuality, family, material sustenance, shelter, food, health, commerce, life, and death. Use your freedom to convey liberty and life to one another. Comfort the afflicted, heal the sick, cast out demons, feed the hungry, and educate the children and those ready to learn even as you carry water to the thirsty. Visit the sick, imprisoned, and dying, move mountains, advocate for the oppressed, raise the dead—live out the template of righteousness—weep with those who weep, mourn with those who mourn, accompany one another in temptation, rejoice with those who rejoice, stand by one another and do not provoke one another or other nations to violence. Paul here is laying out a charter of righteousness and accountability.

The second imperative of the epistle in this portion is about how to be a liberating body even if the time is short. Mourning is not forever, for the Advent Lord is ever-coming so we yearn—"come quickly." Work as if it were just another day, prepare as if it were the last. Maranatha is the Aramaic, Arabic, Syriac—indeed Semitic—plea and prayer that we may be found ready for God's Advent and consummation of all reality.

Pastor Erica's sermon occurs in a period of the life of our church when lively and passionate discussion of sexual theology and ethics is occurring and thoughtful and agonizing debate is occurring around the homosexuality issue. The context is provocative. The Pope today (March 9, 2012) reiterates the Vatican's opposition to "same sex marriage" even as he shores up the church's opposition to contraception, especially as that merges into "morning after" pregnancy prevention and the theologically and ethically profound issue of abortion.

This matter is of enormous moment in Christian sexual bioethics. While my lifelong persuasions on this spectrum of issues feel that the greatest threats to neighbor love are not contraception and homosexuality but heterosexual (and homosexual) child stalking, molestation, and abuse, as well as the "big business" culture of pornography and the homo- and heterosexual vices of incest, rape, violence, promiscuity, and unfaithfulness. The overriding evaluative criterion of biblical faith is simply—"what injures the neighbor?" This is the primary trust committed to our personal, ecclesial, and societal responsibility. To this, of course, must be added the corruptions and debasing evils of sex slavery and trafficking, and the wholesale debasing of conjugal love and caring respect brought about by savage and thoughtless business practices as we buy and sell temptation, seduction, and degradation of persons who are the very image of God in our midst. This is the subject matter of 1 Corinthians 7. The best biblical construal of this biblical material is Ken Bailey's commentary:

> 1 Corinthians 8:
>
> My comments this week are brief and to one central point. Focus on this one revolutionary notion will allow my class to rewind and explore in more depth issues we have passed over in weeks gone by. Since I find this sermon series so outstanding and searching, I am still hoping to publish—probably locally—these sermons and my comments and notes—feeling that the issues broached here go to the quick of the challenges today facing local congregations, Presbyteries, and denominations as well as the global Church and world religion. In Chapter 8, the Apostle gives us one preeminent concept—which is not a concept but a "living power (exousia)"— Scripture's word for energy and authority.
>
> Here it is: The Love of God is the greatest gift in the world (c.f. Ch 13) and that "Gift" comes to life and Spirit in the world as we love one another.
>
> The Pittsburgh Presbyterian School of exegesis (Orr and Walther— then Bailey) put it in this way: "Love is far more important than knowledge. Love for God is more vital than knowledge about him. For Paul—with his deep background in the Torah, knowledge of God would include acceptance of an obedience to God as supreme sovereign." [230, ff Anchor Bible].
>
> They then cite the textus classicus establishing these truths— Exodus 6:7; 10:2; and 18:11, as well as Deuteronomy 29:6.
>
> They continue with the more striking conclusion—that love of God means love of one's neighbors—near and far, and this leads to the realization not that we know God but rather that we have been known by Him! Orr and Walther conclude that the basis of Christian community is the interacting of our love for God and His acceptance of His People. (Remember Tillich's sermon "You Are Accepted"—a great charter of freedom and homecoming for those despised and rejected by the world.

Ken Bailey, with his deep Middle Eastern interpretation of First Corinthians, puts it this way:

> Irresponsible treatment of the brother/sister is a sin against Christ. If we open our heart to know God we then are known by God. In the words of Ch. 13 "we shall know we are known" (13:12). If we think we know autonomously, in the sense of worldly knowing—we deceive ourselves. In the language of John's letters, if we say we love God and hate our neighbors we fool ourselves and the truth is not in us. (1 John 2:1)

This Semitic notion of love as enacted deed is also found in Galatians: "Before you did not know God—only the 'no gods' which are your idols. Now after you have come to know God—or rather become known of God—why do you want to return to bondage . . . all the Law is fulfilled in one word—you shall love your neighbor as yourself" (Gal 4:1—5:14).

The chapter of the day seems to be about true and false knowledge—true and false love. As Calvin concludes, "If we love God we love our neighbors in Him."

VII. SELF-DENIAL, SACRIFICIAL LOVE, REMEMBRANCE, AND PAROCHIAL AND PUBLIC WITNESS, CHAPTER 8

The chapter moves on a Middle Eastern rhetorical arc (see Bailey, p. 243) from my rights through five cameos: soldier, Torah. Scripture, Torah, and plowman—back to my rights reconsidered. The undergirding foundational premise from chapter 8 is that God is God—his emissary Lord is Lord—no other gods or lords matter since they are imaginary. Therefore, Paul is set free as an apostle, and we therefore are set free in apostolic ministry, under obligation, which is our freedom.

The passage from Martin Luther as he and Erasmus debated freedom and ministry is drawn from this text: The Christian is the "perfectly free Lord of all—subject to none. The Christian is the perfectly dutiful servant of all—subject to all" (*The Freedom of a Christian*). The parable picture here is an unyoked, then reyoked, ox. We remember Jesus' counsel—be not unwillingly, inappropriately, and burdensomely yoked (my paraphrase) rather—"take my Yoke upon you and learn of me—my yoke is easy and my burden is light" (Luke 14:19).

Bottom line—now that you are set free from oppression, become servile to God and one another; this is true freedom. The five cameos depict this human service and servitude, later addressed in Paul's hymn in Philippians: "though in the form of God—[infinitely free and powerful] he did not grasp at that equality but emptied himself . . . took on the form of a slave . . . took on humanness and became obedient unto death, even the gruesome death of a cross. Therefore God has highly exalted him" (Phil 2: 6–9). In Bach's cantata of this liturgical week, based on this Kenosis hymn, this passage is put in this way: "*Ertragtsein Kreuzmit Christlicher Gellassenheit.*" He carries his cross with Christlike-abandon, obedience, and serenity. BMW 93.

Let us return to our text for the week, 1 Cor 10:1–13. The passage first appeals to the "faith of our fathers." Moses and the wandering, the ever grumbling chosen people were "baptized" in the sea and the cloud—a fascinating image. They were bewildered as they sojourned in the place of temptation. It was feast or famine in the desert—a strangely unconducive milieu for their journey of faith-formation.

In a hard-to-decipher metaphor—they all ate and drank from the "Rock," which Paul of Damascus says is "Christ," and his Jewish contemporary, Philo of Alexandria, says is Hikma-Sophia, or Wisdom.

Perhaps wilderness temptation is baptism. Our son Keith, a pediatrician, refers to his "baptism of fire" when, as a young doctor in the Navy, he was assigned to Guam as the primary attending physician and a Korean airliner with dozens of children aboard slammed into the back side of Mount Lamlam on the island. Caring day and night for the burned and injured would lead to months of trekking back and forth to Seoul trying to save the tiny victims. Karl Barth said that baptism was like gasping for God as a drowning person gasps for air. The teaching of Paul along the channel of Corinth was of the same tremendum.

In the Abrahamic faiths, baptism, i.e., covenant (fire, water, wind) includes flesh (circumcision), death, drowning, and air (breath). The liturgical moments of this season—suffering (temptation), crucifixion (asphyxiation), dying (release of Spirit), burial (baptism), and resurrection (revival and resuscitation)—range from the days of transfiguration to Pentecost. This is the matrix where release conquers suffering: no overwhelming temptation will overcome you (1 Cor 10:13), life overcomes death and righteousness displaces evil.

The covenants of Isaac, Ishmael, and Jesus—those three Abrahamic and biblical signs and seals—chartered in Torah and prophets—Jesus, Bible, and in Paul (cf, Romans and Galatians), all grow out of Abraham's call and pilgrimage, the oppression and exodus of Jacob/Israel, Moses' theophany—receipt of Verbum Dei—apocalypse and change of the age, the fullness of time, new creation, dawn of redemption, and the culmination of the age. They all involve temptation, the confrontation of good and evil and the vicarage, the vicarious victory of the Messiah within and without the world, the world created for him and for which he came to save. This assertive "faith of the fathers" then remains the central substance of all of us who follow in that faith and life heritage for all ages to come.

The text then moves to a theme that weaves its way through the letter. Liberation and freedom brings on a faith and life characterized by challenge, choice, and temptation. While God has rescued, delivered, and provided for his people, we grumble in ingratitude, and that grumbling soon turns into apostasy (denial of God and neglect of worship), idolatry (service of subprime "no gods"), injustice, and immorality. We choose to violate the vertical and horizontal directions of the covenant. In neglect of our rightful service we turn to serve strange gods and turn God's temple into a den of thieves and God's temple "in us" into a sacrilege.

In verse 7ff., we witness the tragedy of this declension from true faith/life. Idolatry displaces loyalty. Porneia, bodily immorality, harmful relationality, again rears its ugly head. Instead of withstanding our temptation in the allowance and escape plan of God, we commit the ultimate unforgivable sin against the Holy Spirit that is Godself and we tempt Christ. With the Lord of all being still on the cross we shout "come down and we will believe;" "save yourself and us." And 23,000 fall in the desert.

After this interlude on the ultimate powerless of temptation to overwhelm and undo us, the passage turns to a hymn of victory. "We are one bread and one body"—no longer do the prostituted body and sacrilegious bread pertain—we are—through grace—the body of Christ and the blood of Christ. The cup and loaf of blessing that we bless, is it not that very body and blood? We have here the first enunciation of the hallelujah chorus of this holy week and the concluding chapters of this letter, which appears in chapter 11, verse 23—"I deliver unto you that which I also received that on the night . . ."

First Corinthians 10: 25 and 26: "Eat whatever is sold in the meat market—without raising any questions on the ground of conscience . . . For the earth is the Lord's and the fullness thereof"—translation by Ken Bailey in *Paul Through Mediterranean Eyes*.

Our meditation this week is Paul's profound message of our freedom, even amid the responsibilities to which we are bound. Pastor Ray will preach on "Green Theology"—in celebration of Earth Day. For me it is also a landmark week as my dear Sara returns home with a rebuilt right leg, testing the biblical promise that "the lame will walk." Beyond that, I remember Dick Clark, who just died, with an overwhelming broken heart and I remember when I, too, awkwardly maneuvered my teenage body to the latest rock and roll on "American Bandstand" with some of my high school friends in New York City. I must confess as I see Gloria Gaynor paying tribute to Dick, that I prefer another version of "I Will Survive" than that of the "Pug" singing the noble hit while riding the jump seat in the movie *Men in Black II*. Let all creatures join the hope mod!

The apostle here meditates on a leitmotif of his thought, which calls us to see our accountability in this world under God as being "all things to all people." As Bailey reminds us in his commentary on 1 Corinthians, Paul is addressing his specific context of causing offense to any Jew, Greek, or Christian (see p. 284). In our context, this might well mean not wounding the conscience of blacks, Muslims, gays, children, religious conservatives, liberals, or secularists—Republicans or Democrats. In God's richly pluralistic world—made that way in deliberate divine will—it may be said that God is seeking through this medium to further his will and way among all peoples in his beloved world. Why? "For the earth is the Lord's and the fullness thereof" (1 Cor 10:26). The world is rapidly becoming more diverse and though some are profoundly threatened by this development, in our congregation—"thanks be to God"—we are thrilled.

It is the emerging presence of a "new world"—what faith calls the "kingdom"—that is the reason God created this world through the "redeemer/wisdom" (Colossians 1:15—"He is the image of the invisible God, the first-born of all creation—by Him all things were created").

Here is the theological bottom line: Since creation is made for redemption not futility (Romans 8), don't offend the moral sensibilities of others but rather build up one another; gracefully receive and welcome one another, don't tear down and rip apart. Edify the world of God as it arises on your watch, and build up the "body of God."

Which brings us to our sermon of today.

"Green Theology" piques Pastor Ray's thought on this Earth Day. The text of Psalm 104: 10–30 is powerful:

He makes springs pour water into the ravines;
it flows between the mountains.
They give water to all the beasts of the field;
the wild donkeys quench their thirst.
The birds of the sky nest by the waters;
they sing among the branches.
He waters the mountains from his upper chambers;
the land is satisfied by the fruit of his work.
He makes grass grow for the cattle,
and plants for people to cultivate—
bringing forth food from the earth:
wine that gladdens human hearts,
oil to make their faces shine,
and bread that sustains their hearts.
The trees of the LORD are well watered,
the cedars of Lebanon that he planted.
There the birds make their nests;
the stork has its home in the junipers.
The high mountains belong to the wild goats;
the crags are a refuge for the hyrax.
He made the moon to mark the seasons,
and the sun knows when to go down.
You bring darkness, it becomes night,
and all the beasts of the forest prowl.
The lions roar for their prey
and seek their food from God.
The sun rises, and they steal away;
they return and lie down in their dens.
Then people go out to their work,
to their labor until evening.
How many are your works, LORD!
In wisdom you made them all;
the earth is full of your creatures.
There is the sea, vast and spacious,
teeming with creatures beyond number—
living things both large and small.
There the ships go to and fro,
and Leviathan, which you formed to frolic there.
All creatures look to you
to give them their food at the proper time.
When you give it to them,
they gather it up;
when you open your hand,

> they are satisfied with good things.
> When you hide your face,
> they are terrified;
> when you take away their breath,
> they die and return to the dust.
> When you send your Spirit,
> they are created,
> and you renew the face of the ground. (NIV)

My paraphrase:

He sends springs and streams into the mountains and valleys. The animals and birds can drink. He creates scrub-grasses and woods.

For a good portion of our lives and ministries, Pastor Ray and I have walked and run through the woods and streams of western Pennsylvania. We know the therapeutic refreshment of a walk in the woods. Bill Bryson wrote the book (*A Walk in the Woods*) and Robert Redford set out to do the film.

Here are just some of the vivifying and edifying benefits of walks in the woods and what these green fellow creatures and friends offer:

They reduce the impact of poor air quality, global warming;

They absorb pollutants, intercepting smoke, pollen and dust;

They release oxygen for healing and process the trapped heat of urban centers;

They have restorative and creative effects on the mind;

They show us our place on the good earth and therefore our giftedness in the provision of God.

But these woods are not accessible to the vast majority of peoples on God's "good earth." The forests are rapidly disappearing—from North Carolina's pine forests, to the Amazon rain forests (which Brazil's president says the world should pay for so that earth can continue to breathe), to the virgin Hemlock and hardwoods of western Pa. These woods of my and Ray's deep memory and thanksgiving are now an epicenter of the world's frantic search for coal, oil, and gas. Presbyterians like Carnegie and Mellon were at the forefront of their exploitation and of the attempt to bring good from their productive yield.

Today waste-water burial and fracking raise new scenarios of earthquake and employment, good and evil—justice and greed. This earth is not ours to slash and burn but to tend, garden, and be good stewards. It is an uncanny relation so close to what I first learned about the God-relation in the Calvin catechism in those hills and on those streams: What is the chief end of man?—Man's chief end is to glorify God and enjoy him forever. In a few weeks I will return to these Pennsylvania homelands weeping and rejoicing with those who do the same—as Paul admonishes.

X. STIGMATA, RESURRECTION LOGIC, AND COSMIC TRANSFIGURATION, CHAPTER 13

Good Friday, Easter Sunday, Easter Evening: 1 Corinthians 15:

Experience is exciting and enigmatic. My Sara is in rehab following a knee replacement and reconstruction. At morning prayers with the "old boys" at church and a moving speaker—of Evanston Township High School, Nebraska, and pro football fame, now awaiting a kidney transplant and hobbling along on bad knees—I remembered that on Holy Friday and Saturday, Jesus took broken legs (John 19:32), an expended body, and many wounds into the tomb to go to work to gather all wounded and broken humanity into his cosmic self in Easter resurrection. Much whirls through the mind—broken bones, quiet, but painful, healing, "Beloved Son" (Isaiah 53 and Psalm 89). "Pastor Blood" (a phlebotomist pastor from the Church of God in North India led us in prayer after drawing blood—his day job)—myriad impressions!

Commentary:

Here's the question underlying the flurry of experience: "How on earth did Jesus become a God?" (Larry Hortado, *How on Earth Did Jesus Become a God?* Grand Rapids, MI: Eerdmans, 2005.)

The question is problematic in itself since there can be (1) no other God but God—the Al' Shaddah of Islam and likely early Jewish Christianity; (2) the Great Shemah of biblical Israel—"Hear O Israel—the Lord our God is One . . . you shall have no other gods"; and (3) Jesus' own insistence "Why do you call me good . . . there is none good but God" (Luke 18:19). These attestations are the most fundamental premises of all three monotheistic, Abrahamic, and biblical faiths. "Good news" or the "Gospel of God" (Romans 1)—what the New Testament calls "Kerygma" (proclamation)—is the way that Easter faith seeks to explain "our knowledge of the unknown God" or in better phrasing—"How we are being and becoming known to the unknown God?"

First Corinthians 15 is a very early formulation of this gospel and the heart and essence of that gospel. Paul articulates it in awesome theological and hermeneutical phrasing:

> I delivered to you what I had received—that Christ died for our sins according to the scriptures; that he was buried and that he was raised on the third day according to the scriptures; and that he appeared to Peter and the twelve. (1 Cor 15:3–5)

The Pauline version had some predecessors such as "Jesus is Lord" (Phil 2:11) and later versions—all of which work with the Greek word *Christos*, which renders the Hebrew, Aramaic, and Arabic *Mashiah*, the Anointed.

The first creed developed in this way:

On Palm Sunday, we noted that an anointed king in the tradition of Messiah was celebrated. Notions swirled in the expectancy abroad in the land that he would be a warrior, a liberator, a savior—a new king to set Israel free from the Roman imperial occupation. He was coming in the tradition of King David. He was God's own beloved son who would, in the terms of Psalm 89, set the oppressed people free. But from the beginning, his mission takes on a different guise. There is a deeper wisdom afoot rather than a furtive and futile military escapade. But it was the oxymoron—the absolute contradiction to those who didn't get it—a suffering savior, a dying Mashiah.

Paul's contemporary, Philo of Alexandria, spiritualized the whole thing. He believed that Messiah—Logos—Word—Wisdom—was coeternal with God Eternal. He likely thought of the coming of the "King of the Jews," in the unlikely possibility that he noticed the fracas in Jerusalem that Passover, as some continuum with eternal wisdom, Hickmah. Sometimes this "coming One" was conceived as a "second God" in heaven. In pious expectation, he was thought of as Emmanuel—a gentle one making his hard way to squeeze himself into this world to come and be with us forever. He was called Christos, Messiah, Word, Wisdom, Way, Isaac, Torah. Bottom line—Godself had come to the earth, became like us, died our death, rose our rising, and left behind his Paraclete-teacher to be with us on the earth forever—while he sat reigning on his Davidic throne forever. When Barth was asked by his friend Thurneysen how he was dying with such peace, Barth replied, "*Ersitz in regiment*"—He reigns.

There are three excellent books on this critical subject: Jon Levenson's *The Death and Resurrection of the Beloved Son*; Larry Hortado's *Lord Jesus Christ*; and Paul Van Buren's, *According to the Scriptures*.

The essence of the story was the "death and resurrection" of Jesus and how that story became Gospel proclamation—a new articulation of an old story about the meaning of "all that is." The proclamation was in the Old Testament. This was the only Scripture that Jesus knew. The story is told by a small band of Jews—soon to be derisively called Christians—of one Christos, anointed one, King in the line of David, a savior (healer, liberator) like Yahweh, a Lord (Kurios) like a conquering ruler who took out the enemies as had happened with Egypt, Babylon, Assyria, and now Rome was next. Here Paul is interesting because he seems to believe that Rome is a divinely sanctioned conqueror and empire (Romans 12).

In Jesus language, kingdom is realm, kin-dom or kingdom of God. As Easter approaches, when my dear Sara goes into and recovers from her surgery, I whisper to her of the new order where "the lame walk" and the deer "leaps in dancing." A literary person, she gets those pictures. On Easter morning I hear my favorite hymn of the day, one which depicts this ethical realm, a realm of righteousness: "Easter morn, Easter morn, give to all the forlorn—for *Christ the Lord Is Arisen*. . . those who love freely give, long and well may they live—for *Christ the Lord Is Arisen*." First Corinthians 15 is about emblematic and proleptic righteousness. Not yet fully realized except in sign and promise—it is here—for good.

So, in sum, this is the king nobody wanted. Popular expectations were dashed. A complete contrarian showed up. A Savior, Lord, King—so unlike what we wanted:

He comes riding a nursing donkey trailing the foal—Alexander the Great's warhorse (see Zechariah 9). No way!

What we see is Genesis 22 reenacted; the son(s) Isaac and Ishmael are being offered as "beloved sons." Jeshua Mashiah, only in triumphalist images of one hundred years later, Jesus Christ, Paul's premonition, is *monogenos* and *agapetos* (only begotten and beloved) in the image of Isaiah 53, wounded for our iniquities and healing with these wounds.

In the images of 2 Samuel: "I will be his father and he will be my son" and in the controlling language of Psalm 89 (alluded to twenty times in Christian Scripture): "I have found David my Son. With my holy oil I have anointed him . . . The enemy will not harm him or the wicked afflict him. I will set his hands on the seas and rivers. He will cry to me—'You are my father and my God—my rock "Hikmah'" [Wisdom/Philo]. And I will make him my first-born, higher than all of the kings on earth. His seed will endure forever" (Ps 89: 20–28)

All this is gathered by Paul into one glorious, realized expectation (*en Christou*). Christ suffered, died, was buried, rose, appeared . . . according to the scriptures—and at last to me (1 Cor 15: 3–4).

Another way of comprehending the Easter/empty tomb narrative— this founding drama of our faith—embracing the suffering, dying, rising, appearing, ascending, and reigning of the beloved son (John 3:16) is found in the earliest catechism ritual known in the early church: what is known as the Doctrine of Faith in Hippolytus (see Ed Phillips contribution to the *Hermeneia Commentary Series*, Minneapolis: Augsburg Fortress, 2002). Here is the narrative:

In the late first century as the faith was assuming formulation (credo) and structure, the Hypopolitan doctrinal text emerges as the first menu of Christian catechesis. Novices in the faith concluded their intensive prayer, learning, and preparation during Easter week. As dawn broke and the Easter sun rose, the neophyte expressed her faith. It was a life and death assertion especially in those ages of persecution. After the catechetical points of credo, the culminating question was raised before the life or death symbol of baptism occurred. "What are you going to do about the widows and orphans?" [personal communication from Ed Phillips]. Here we see the integral connection between the Human-God vector and the human-human vector.

Nov 3, 2012—Staten Island

Another of the floating islands and marshes we call New York City and New Jersey. Governor Cuomo calls it the "once in a hundred years storm which comes every two years." "Global warming?" "Hush, don't say it." A saintly blind woman with her seeing-eye poodle feels the anguish even though she can't see it. She'll cook up some food and with her co-opted friends, she will set it out on tables in the street. And the hash and chips suddenly becomes an overflowing smorgasbord—and a few bread and fishes become a feast. And the Messianic bread of life, *Panis Angelicus*, is present as we lovingly care for each other. Soon shipments from cars, busses, trains, and planes pour in and the poor, homeless John Candy receives Thanksgiving and dinner.

Part 2

Eight

Election Countdown

Saturday and Sunday, November 3 and 4.

THE ELECTION DRAWS NEAR. Two irregularities are already pronounced. At least 68 to 69 percent of white males in the country are voting for Romney (or against Obama). Something has taken place in our culture that precipitates this unprecedented event. Whites, especially white males, exhibit an intense animus against the president and the reason remains enigmatic and suppressed. Is it racism, party-loyalty, fear that he is an alien, Muslim, socialist, or some other "*other*"? Secondly, an article in *Tikkun* magazine calls for an emergency process that should come from the national legislature, the state attorney generals, or the U.S. Supreme Court (were not these bodies so implicated and complicit in these abridgements of fundamental human rights). Obama, the inveterate compromiser, can't or won't do it. I know him too well! The drumbeat of racial "othering," anathematizing and disenfranchisement, goes on and on. An op-ed in the November 14, 2012 edition of *Tikkun*, "Obama Must Use Military to Ensure a Free and Fair Election" provides evidence.

> "Wrongful Life cannot be Right."
> —Theodore Adorno

Election Day: November 6, 2012.

In the early morning hours today, after a short game of hoops near our former Hyde Park neighborhood, where we often crossed paths with Barack, Michelle, and the tiny girls, the president shared these stirring words:

> This world moves forward because of you. It moves forward because you reaffirmed the spirit that has triumphed over war and depression, the spirit that has lifted this country from the depths of despair to the great heights of hope, the belief that while each of us will pursue our own individual dreams, we are an American family and we rise or fall together as one.

Election Day Eve: November 5, 2012:

Early in this book, I predicted that this election would be 50.1 to 49.9 percent—one way or the other. And so it appears today. And pain and anger and that enervated feeling that we have been bamboozled by what seems to be countless politicians, pollsters, pundits, pay-rollers, and other partisans—is all around. We are weary and tomorrow's conclusion to the whole gruesome and embarrassing mess will be a relief.

My Post-Election Comments:

Pew research in election exit polls enriched by general post-election probes finds many unsettling facts:

- The election was very negative. More attacks, lying, and distortion gave many a "throw all the bums out" attitude.
- The press gets very bad grades (D and F).
- 70 percent of the people want compromise but doubt whether that is forthcoming.
- People are incensed that the media's toleration of dishonesty has let it "get out of hand."
- The entire campaign was "devoid of substance" and "big money" has corrupted the entire election process. Most believe that many government programs work well, though we should work through local and private sector processes if at all possible.
- Most believe that health care (e.g., Medicare and Medicaid) can best be presented by public policy systems rather than by private business insurance companies.

- The creative genius of this and any society is the synergic interplay of all of the spheres of life organization—for profit, not for profit, public, state, individual, corporations. Grover Norquist saying he wants to reduce government to the size of a bathtub where he can "drown" it. One wonders if the nation is as mad and destructive as he is.

Context and Assumptions of My Reflections:

In the late 1960s, when I was doing my doctoral studies in Germany, we were attracted by a program in the Cologne Cathedral entitled *"Politische Nachtgebet"* ("Political Vespers"). The services drew thousands of persons engaging the deep liturgies, prayers, songs, and Scriptures of the German churches—Roman Catholic, Reformed, and Lutheran—to address the agonizing public issues of the day: post war recovery in Germany, the Vietnam War, Russian occupation of Eastern Europe, economics and the breakdown of human justice, and neighborliness in the war-ravaged culture.

The leader of the effort was a distinguished theologian, Dorothee Soelle, one of the first great women theologians of the German church and university, who had been trained in the field of philosophy and literature. As a young doctoral scholar, I was working on the issues of systematic theology and social ethics as these arose in the context of Nazi technology and medicine, especially of the medical atrocities and the Holocaust, along with the broader issues of emerging cybernetic technologies (i.e., extending the human sensorium: thought, sight, hearing, bodily organs, and functions) through computers, cyborg devices, robotic systems, and general amplification of human power through electric extension.

Those "Political Vespers" not only helped me formulate the theological problems but gave me a model of expansive interfaith theology and ethics, and a correlational methodology (rising from the new voices in Germany: Rahner, Kung, Thielicke, Tillich, Pannenberg, Moltmann, and others). These all sought to relate biblical theology and ethics to these compelling cultural issues. I accepted the Jewish dictum that the Holocaust was an event in biblical history.

Nine

Obama and Romney Election Night Speeches

Election Evening, November 6, 2012.

A surprising and impressive victory for Obama: 50 percent to 49 percent, 3 million plurality, with a big electoral edge at 330–206.

November 7, 2012.

GOVERNOR ROMNEY SPOKE IN a chastened mood—still oblivious to the terrible mendacity of the narrative of failure about Obama that he and his handlers concocted to attack the president. Let us hope that his message of contrition brings about forgiveness and, more important, brings resolve to seek reconciliation across our divisions as we settle in to concretely work creatively to tackle the enormous crisis agenda that we face.

He and his family are rooted in a faith posture, which I have chronicled earlier in this memoir, and indeed will be part of the foundation of justice and kindness upon which rebuilding can begin. His words, spoken over the protests of Mr. Karl Rove on Fox News, promote healing. I am especially moved and challenged by the good words he has for teachers, theologians, and spiritual leaders in this world. Would he only see through his blinders (and binders) and see that his opponent was one of the very special and chosen of this cadre of moral leaders in God's world at this time. See my book on the 2008 election: *America in God's World* (Wipf and Stock, 2009). See also Romney's concession speech, found in the November 7, 2012 edition of the Washington Post, sec. 1, 6.; and Obama's victory speech, found in the November 7, 2012 edition of the Washington Post, sec. 1, 5.

My Comments:

The thoughts of our two aspiring leaders sketch out an agenda of beliefs, values, actions, and policies which can be sketched out for examination as we summarize this portentous day . . .

We believe in freedom and duty.
We believe in individuality and community.
We believe in opportunity and equality.

We value health and home, work and leisure, adequate wealth to sustain the life entrusted to us and to care for others. We seek these values for all. We value the rights of all and of "the least of these."

We, therefore, form policies and develop programs to provide health care for all, to provide homes, work, support for children and the old; to provide security and peace at home and abroad; to create government that sees the higher value of helping those who have too little, not those who have too much. Government should not generate dependence but help all become independent and self-sustaining. Women's rights and needs should be a high priority for the public and legal policy of any jurisdiction.

Ten

Rachel Maddow's Election Litany

Wednesday, Nov 7, 2012.

Rachel Maddow delivered a litany on the results of the election which aired on MSNBC November 7, 2012 during *The Rachel Maddow Show*:

> After marriage rights for same-sex couples were voted down in state after state after state for years, more than 30 times in a row, this year, all change in Maine; they voted on marriage equality and they voted for it.
> In Maryland, they voted on marriage equality and they voted for it.
> In Minnesota, they were asked to vote against marriage equality, and Minnesota refused to ban it.
> In Iowa, anti-gay activists were sure that they were going to turf out a judge for ruling in favor of marriage equality. They had done it before, to a bunch of other judges. They had been successful every time they had tried before, but not this one, not this time. Judge Wiggins in Iowa keeps his seat.
> Nevada elects its first African American congressman this year.
> America gets our first openly gay United States senator.
> America gets our first-ever Asian American woman senator from Hawaii.
> California relaxed its "three strikes you're out" law and rejected a law to cripple the power of unions.
> Decriminalization of marijuana was approved in Washington and in Colorado.
> More women got elected to the U.S. Senate than at any time in U.S. history.

The Republican presidential nominee and vice presidential nominee both lost their home states.

And, oh, yes, this happened. President Barack Obama, yes, will go down in history as our nation's first African American president. But he will also go down in history as the most successful Democratic presidential candidate since FDR.

The polls were right, even without Florida being decided, we now know that President Obama won in pretty much exactly the way the state-by-state polls said he was going to win. He won with more than 300 electoral votes. It was not magic, it was just math. Math that was completely invisible to the political right.

My Comment: The Stanford and Oxford graduate (Rhodes Scholar) is a liturgist, par excellence. She is one of the bright stars who has emerged on the political firmament. Praises and Prayers—as we Protestants would have it.

I have two moments of pause in the otherwise jubilant response for Obama: (1) He was too ruthless and relentless in his critique of his predecessor, George "W" Bush. The global economic crisis was in part accountable to his "credit card" assumption of two unpaid-for wars and the massive tax cut for the hyper-wealthy—"those who have too much." But the global downturn was budding in America—probably under Reagan and was part of a natural, cyclic phenomenon, and (2) His blaming McCain for Bush was not right and his constant maligning of Romney—especially the summer endeavor to paint him as a rich, uncaring, Bain vulture capitalist was one-sided, self-righteous, and distorted. Obama's handlers openly admitted, belatedly, that this was a carefully premeditated and crafted attempt to "define" Romney for the nation and world before he could define himself—still reeling from the bloody primaries. Shame!

In the election aftermath, it has become clear that "Obama for America" threw a fist-full of bucks into the creation of this "straw-man." As for me, I am thankful that both of these decent, just, and kind persons were willing to set aside their comfortable careers—become "hard as nails" with "the constitution of an ox and the skin of a Rhinoceros," as Rowan Williams said, referring to what will be needed in the new Archbishop of Canterbury—and become willing to be public servants whose hair will rapidly whiten.

Obviously, as we scan Rachel's litany, the election was a moral victory for the forces of right and good. Now will we find here a call for reconciliation and concerted edifying action for our struggling nation and the world.

My Comment: This statistical litany also discloses an ominous fact. Exit polls by Edison Research (*New York Times*, Nov. 10, 2010, A19) show that white males voted against Obama—65% in California, 66% in Colorado, 65% in Illinois, 67% in Maryland, 66% in Michigan, 67% in Nevada, New Mexico 69%, Ohio 69%, Pennsylvania 68%, Virginia 73%, and Florida 73 %. These are all states won by Obama and given the fact that black, Latino, and Asian males are known to have supported Obama in greater proportion in those states, the ratio of white males against Obama is probably greater—perhaps over 70%. These data make us look like apartheid South Africa or the postbellum South or dare I say, National Socialist Germany. Not only can we "white guys" not jump, we are a national disgrace. Did I hear correctly that more blacks voted in this election for Obama than whites? This lopsided see-saw of ethnic balancing surely portends some pathology or at least racism.

Thursday, November 8, 2012.

Gabby Gifford's colleague, Ron Barber, has narrowly won the election in Congressional District Two in Arizona. A loss would have been an amazing snub—of a world-renowned leader and her chosen successor, before a watching international audience from a state that seems to live in the twilight zone between "deep sea tea" and some semblance of civility. Return to your seat soon, Gabby! Godspeed! Gabby and Mark are in court today to answer questions in a hearing for her attempted murderer—Jared Loughner (see my book *While I Have Being: Winterreise (Winter Journey*, Wipf and Stock, 2012, section: "Tucson Ordeal").

My updates on this case are several. In attempting to fathom the lineaments of good and evil—the theological underpinnings of secular justice and mercy, I raised questions such as:

Should the victims have mercy on the perpetrator of this ghastly crime even in the face of the prevailing environment toward Gabby within which he was "acting out"?

Should he be "drug treated" for the schizophrenia, which obviously precipitated his action, so that being found temporarily sane, he could be given the death sentence (capital punishment) or at least a life sentence?

How do we find redemption and closure within the terror of this circumstance?

Why are some places in the world pro-death sentence when other places have banned such? Is there some underlying religiocultural impulse behind each of these public policy options? (e.g, Texas and Vermont—Scandinavia and the United States?).

How can we prevent such brutality (mass killings by insane persons with easy access to guns), which obviously concentrates in some places and not others?

Eleven

Booklet on 2008 Election

"The Chicago Two and Old Mac"

My pamphlet on the 2008 election (previously unpublished document), along with the book, *America in God's World* (Wipf and Stock, 2009), cover the penultimate election as this year's election pamphlet, as I campaigned in Indiana, Pennsylvania, and Wisconsin, as I had for the just-completed campaign in the accompanying pamphlet.

Dateline: January 31, 2008.

Kodak Auditorium, Los Angeles

The "cesspool" [sic] (press-pool) of paparazzi depart from the orchestra pit after the flurry of photo-flashes.

Two faces appear—remarkably different from all previous presidential presentations—a woman and an African American—take their seats.

The debate begins:

> Hillary Rodham Clinton:
>
>> . . . we must achieve universal health care. In this most gifted and blessed nation, it is a moral right for people to have accessible and affordable health care.
>>   . . . we need access in cities and rural areas. We spend more than any other nation in the world and vast numbers still do not receive health care.
>>   . . . we must provide rather than impede solutions for global warming and environmental stewardship.

... we must not condemn or hound down those who seek work in this country. The House of Representatives recently passed such an inhuman and harsh law that would have penalized the Good Samaritan and Jesus Christ himself.

Barack Hussein Obama:

... the nation is at war, the planet is in peril, we must move in a new direction.

... we must decrease the influence of lobbyists and special interests. I will bring ethics back into Washington politics.

Let us end this misguided war. We must never again commit the lives of our young women and men unless it is last resort, has a clear goal, results from a proven attack against us and has a transparent entrance and exit strategy.

... we have a moral obligation to see that everyone in this country who wants it can get health care. Those of us who are fortunate and blessed should shoulder the burden of the sick, poor, aged, and weak.

MY APPROACH, E.G., THE ECONOMY

Pregnant and provocative observations and assertions. But what is the bedrock of these beliefs and values—of faith and life—of conviction and conscience? What is the ground from which these political views and actions arise?

Take for example the issues of "the economy," "taxes," and "immigration." Although the political rhetoric euphemistically refers to these as matters of survival, well-being, perhaps even fairness, justice and sacrifice, they are actually patterns of human self-interest, exploitation, and violence.

In other words, they reveal the ambiguous human condition of injustice and justice under the pressures of temptation, good and evil—the subject matter of theology and theological ethics.

The issues, in other words, push back to theological formulations— what Doug Meeks calls the "Economy of Go" and theologian Steve Long, the "Divine Economics."

The cache of issues concern divine providence and the requirements of righteousness. They speak of human generosity and greed, the yearnings of human hope and need. They concern human eschatological expectations where people "will no longer put up with things as they are but chafe under oppression because the goad of the promised future stabs inexorably into every unfulfilled present" (Jurgen Moltmann, *Theology of Hope*, p. 21, 22, Philadelphia: Fortress Press, 1967).

Take two features of the impending economic crisis. On the one hand, the burst bubbles of high-tech stocks and sub-prime mortgages reflect necessary and inevitable periodic global cycles. At the same time, they also reflect economic theologies of "savage capitalism" where some sectors discard common sense and equilibrium and seek rapid and excessive profits. This is true in America now in medicine, law, investment banking, energy, drug and insurance corporations, professional sports, university endowments, and other areas where vested interests seek to race ahead of the modest appreciation that the "common good" and "natural law" allows in order to make exceptional rates of profit even though it causes distress and harm in other sectors of the *oikumene*: our world house where our task must be one of mutual edification.

On the eve of the above cited presidential debate, for example, when oil prices sat near $100 per barrel and poor workers were unable to drive to work, Exxon, the Texas-based oil company, announced exorbitant profits of forty-plus billions. Rather than following the God of justice and sharing, we pursued the idolatries of Friedman economics: "charge (gouge) as much as the market will bear."

COMMENTARY

Is nature and history—matter and time—infinitely plastic to human manipulation and programming or is it contoured by "limits," "givens," and tenored by principles and equilibrium (balances)? Is our theology of time one of "rush," "surge," and infinite pliability to human coercion or are there patterns and quarantines that impose the regularities and wisdom of "chronos" and "kairos"—intrinsic, inherent patterns mediating possibility and sanction?

Critical theology has offered normative renditions of the divine meanings and dynamics of space and time by fathoming the will and action of the divine spirit that animates those realms of reality. Thinkers ranging from Ernst Troeltsch to Max Weber and H. R. Niebuhr have shown that a divine providence permeates space-time, a nature-history process bringing political effect and certain kinds of societies out of the dymamics of Spirit and into the world. The "Chicago Two" lift such realizations into public discourse.

In sum, the subliminal messages of our presidential candidates and the subtle implications of the policy issues at stake point toward deeper theological and ethical dimensions. This essay will seek to lift those up—to delineate and evaluate these implicit but seldom explicated dimensions.

TALE OF TWO CHURCHES: HILLARY

To focus on spiritual and ethical sublimities beneath political phenomena calls our attention to a tale of two churches. Hillary Clinton's campaign popularity with "down-scale," "blue-collar," working people in California, New York, and Pennsylvania can be traced to proclivities rising from her Wesleyan heritage. Though Max Weber places the Methodists within the upwardly mobile Puritan ethos, the "people called Methodists" (since the Wesley brothers nascent ministries in early industrial England) have exemplified the Sermon on the Plain's dictum: "Blessed are you poor, yours is the Kingdom of God" (Luke 6:20). In Somerset and the western counties and on the farms and fields, Wesleyans have shown the world an inspiring care for social justice and the poor.

American congregations perpetuate this heritage. The Rodham home church in Chicago's inner suburb, Park Ridge, and Hillary's activity in youth ministry on various mission projects throughout the Midwest, is acknowledged as a theological source of her political convictions and commitments.

As I study the formative church experiences of Hillary Clinton, I think I understand her. Though I am a decade older, we are both latter-day Puritan Calvinists, persons who envision and evaluate the world in terms of righteous expectations, initially oppressive but ultimately progressive. We are persons who set out to make these dreams happen, even though that often involves an unbecoming audacity. My nurture occurred in a nouveau-riche suburb of New York City as a Calvinist-Presbyterian, hers in Chicago as a Calvinist-Methodist. Although I came of age in the 1950s and Hillary did so in the 1960s, nonetheless we both envisioned a new and better world where personal and societal wrongs might actually be set right through pathways of discipline and human service.

The spiritual landmarks of our adolescence and early adulthood are typical of the America of the last Puritans. Despite the embarrassments of passive-oppressive fathers and surprisingly far-out moms, Hillary (and I) learned from (and were encouraged by) paternal preachments against which we learned the courage of protest and resistance.

She was a Republican soul, as was common in the suburbs of Eisenhower's America. She ventured, even as had her dad, in holy rectitude into the big city of Chicago one night, crossing over the red line of Howard Street—as wayward husbands of Woman's Christian Temperance Union (WCTU) Evanston often would to imbibe—not only to decry that debauchery and drunkenness but, like other smug Republican Puritans, to check on vote fraud in Daley's "vote early and often" city of the "big shoulders."

Like her mom, Hillary was an activist at the Methodist church in Park Ridge. Both were on the altar guild and were Sunday school teachers. Hugh Rodham worked in lace, reminiscent of his Welsh and English forebears who were likely in mining and textile work, knowing the tedium, danger, and ability it provided to realize Wesley's dictum to "make all you can, save all you can, give all you can." Deep in his conscience and sub-consciousness was Wesley's ministry in mines, factories, and fields, and his teaching of the Protestant work ethic. Hillary, I believe, was inculcated somehow by Wesley's compassion for child-workers, working moms, perhaps even the justice and compassion of the German Calvinist pastor's son, Friedrich Engels, in his treatise on working conditions in the lace factories and garment mills of Liverpool where the little nimble fingers of children were exploited and where Wesley demanded adequate diets, hygiene, orange juice—saying that "cleanliness was next to godliness." That she began her public ministry in the child advocacy field with Marian Edelman points in this direction.

A very significant theological departure in Hillary's life occurs in the early sixties when Don Jones, a twenty-six-year old Methodist ordained out of Drew Divinity School, came to be youth pastor at Park Ridge. Jones immediately confronted, and was confronted by, Hillary. She was challenged and confirmed by Don's sermons at the twice weekly meeting called "the University of Life." Confronted by Bob Dylan and the Beatles' theologically provocative songs, Picasso's paintings ("Guernica"), the poetry of E. E. Cummings and T. S. Eliot, and the best of recent theology, hot out of seminary, the young people of this era were challenged to form new religious and ethical world views. Here they were intrigued by the synthetic social justice and evangelical theology of Wesley, Reinhold Niebuhr, and Dietrich Bonhoeffer. Just down Dempster Street in Evanston, Illinois, T. S. Eliot had joined Karl Barth and Garrett professors in formulating the document, "Christ, the Hope of the World," the working document of the global Conference of the World Council of Churches, held in the fifties at Garrett Seminary, Northwestern University, and throughout the city churches. Fresh thought and radical commitment was in the air as it now is in the world in this election year of 2008. Around this nexus of church life, in work projects, youth conferences with black and Hispanic churches, Hillary reflected, "we walked with, talked with, studied and argued with God" (Carl Bernstein, *A Woman in Charge*, New York: Vintage, 2008, p. 30)

Hillary had joined with her dad decrying Mayor Daley's "rigging" of the 1960 election of John F. Kennedy. I had, meanwhile, been removed from my parish in Pittsburgh (something like Don Jones's Park Ridge) for being in jail in Mississippi for freedom and voter-registration marches, and was now exiled to "None Dare Call It Treason"–John Birch Society Illinois. I had been permanently derailed, with most of my fellow priests, ministers, and rabbis of those turbulent years of the early sixties, from our onward march to "big-steeple churches," because of our commitments against the Vietnam War and the racial apartheid in the southlands of America and Africa. Lasting theological convictions and ethical commitments were formed during those agonizing years—in the clergy and among their young protégées in the parishes. During that poignant span of a few years, John Kennedy and his brother, Robert, were assassinated; four little girls were killed by a bomb as they attended Sunday school at Sixteenth Street Baptist Church in Birmingham, Alabama; Martin Luther King was killed in Memphis; and John McCain was shot down and imprisoned in Hanoi, North Vietnam.

A decisive spiritual and ethical event associated with church life was a field trip to the Chicago Sunday Evening Club in the early 1960s to hear the young pastor from the Methodist Boston University, now preacher and civil-rights leader in Georgia—Martin Luther King Jr. The young pastor from Watseka was there in the enthralled congregation somewhere near the teenage dishwater blonde from Park Ridge.

King's sermon was entitled "Remaining Awake through a Great Revolution." The young martyr-theologian, in what I've always thought his best sermon, spoke of a new age that was dawning—an age where judgment and renewal draws near as human malice and violence provokes the justice and mercy of God. "Now this nation and the entire world will stand before the great God of history," he intoned. He then portrayed the great separation of the sheep and goats at the surprising (to both groups) last judgment in Matthew 26:

> For I was hungry and you didn't feed me,
> Thirsty and you gave me no drink,
> Naked and you didn't cloth me,
> Homeless and you did not take me in.

One of the few books Hillary took with her to Wellesley for her freshman fall of 1965 was Barry Goldwater's *Conscience of a Conservative*. I had just completed my first year as Presbyterian pastor in rural Watseka, Illinois, where one year earlier we had finagled what proved to be the only Democratic votes in the precinct by pleading, as new residents, to overlook the residency requirement, offering convincing but deceiving words to the county registrar: "It will be a close election and we will need every vote we can get." Everyone in Watseka knew the source of those two votes for Lyndon Johnson against Barry Goldwater that November.

In her satchel as they drove the big shiny Cadillac out to Massachusetts for Hillary's freshman orientation was a subscription to *Motive* magazine, a Nashville publication that Don Jones had secured for the graduates, and was on our coffee table in Watseka. The wonderful journal joined avant-garde poetry and literature with thoughts from the likes of Bonhoeffer, Carl Michaelsen, and other theological pioneers—convictions always related to social justice. Don Jones would continue to be a close confidante and adviser when Hillary became a young political leader at Wellesley. In her hours of doubt and loneliness, he passed along Tillich's sermon, "You Are Accepted." She began, through Don's pastoral care, to sense the coexistence and synergy of sin and grace. His admonition also spurred and supplied her Puritan convictions and blessed assurance that our souls are saved as sheer unmerited grace animates Godly hard work and good works. By her college years, she was confirmed in the cache of deep Wesleyan convictions and commitments: civil rights, women's rights and powers, concerns for children, the sick and poor. These would deepen and broaden in the trying and thrilling experiences of Little Rock, Washington D.C. (ethicist Phil Wogaman's preaching), and New York City.

Home from college in August of 1968, Hillary observed with horror the infamous Democratic National Convention and Grant Park demonstrations across Michigan Avenue from the Hilton Hotel, when the horses, tear gas, and dogs were unleashed against the Chicago Seven and other demonstrators, and when Mayor Richard M. Daley had the mike turned off on Senator Ribicoff before the millions watching around the world when he dared decry the "police-state" that gripped Chicago. We were scant comforted with Mayor Daley's malapropism that the police were not there (at the Convention Hotel) "to cause disorder but to maintain disorder." Now we can only ask, in the post 9/11 security state, whether the frightful atmosphere would still be there when the Democrats gather, forty years later—this time in Denver. Revulsion led Hillary to cut her Republican ties forever, and a new theological awareness fashioned a kind of populist Democratic commitment that is still being refined. Along with a few Democrats, she can be found at congressional prayer breakfasts as well as meetings of the congressional black caucus.

BARACK OBAMA

Trinity United Church of Christ is a self-proclaimed "unabashedly black and unapologetically Christian congregation." With a curriculum and *kerygma* of mingled black pride, cultural iconoclasm, evangelical faith, and service to the community, she has become the nurturing fellowship for Michelle and Barack Obama and the girls—the primary source of Barack's theology, ethics, and rhetorical virtuosity.

Faith begins, as with most of us, in the arms, acknowledging the face and voice, of a devoted and devout mother—"the most spiritually awakened person I'd ever known" (*Audacity of Hope*, New York: Vintage, p. 205). For Barack, a vibrant and open viewpoint is directly attributable to that most remarkable mother. If, as Nobel laureate Amartya Sen claims, authentic faith is heterodox, tolerant, and argumentative, he drank this disposition in at the bosom of his anthropologist mom who taught that all religion should be treated with "suitable respect . . . and suitable detachment" (p. 204).

She also exposed him to Buddhism and other world religions, Catholicism and Islam (with the help of his similarly agnostic father).

Barack was to undergo determinative experiences with negative theology: the perennial doorway to faith, where idol busting (e.g., self-adulation, country, prosperity, success) precedes the positive theology of knowledge and righteousness. After working for a consortium of South

Side Chicago churches amid the poverty, unemployment, and discouragement of the wasteland of crumbled factories and steel mills, he underwent a religious awakening at Trinity and was baptized. Today, he humbly and gratefully finds himself a convicted and convinced Christian apostle and public service missionary which, in part, explains his appeal to that evangelical population that was previously the exclusive dominion of the Republican Party.

His is a truly remarkable theological pilgrimage and present witness. His Muslim-raised father distanced himself both from fanatic Islam and from witch-doctor mumbo-jumbo in the Kenyan village of his youth. His grandfather's family were practicing Methodists who exemplified the piety that is so dynamic in Hillary Clinton's story. In his five-year sojourn in Indonesia, Barack was exposed to Buddhist, Catholic, and Islamic rituals and education, planting the seeds for seeing beyond facile theology of all sorts through to authentic universal faith and ethics. Suharto, and Suharto expediencies, we may hope, were exchanged in his soul and spirit for the worldview of Bangladeshi Nobelist, Muhammad Yunus, a disposition of unceasing compassion toward the poor and sick of the earth.

Barack's pastor, Jeremiah Wright, is a regular teacher at our seminary. I have learned from these lectures and from my many students who are assistant pastors in Trinity parish that his is a most unique theological formation. Trained at the University of Chicago in philosophy, theology, and Islam, his aniconic flare and substance is far from your standard liberal-church fare. Theologians in the church, like Dwight Hopkins, Linda Thomas, and my students meet in that throbbing pulpit a Howard Thurman, a Martin Luther King Jr.-style public intellectual with great sagacity, artistic power, and an ever-troublesome, radical biblical Christocentricity and totally innovative modernity. Jeremiah, and the formative congregation that sustained him, surrounded and superintended the baptism, the death, and the rising of Barack Obama into an Augustinian boldness tenored by historical acumen and rhetorical ease.

As one reads *The Audacity of Hope*, the title taken from one of Jeremiah Wright's sermons, along with the many other biographies, we find other spiritual/moral landmarks that will mark the career geography of this one-time editor of the Harvard Law Review. These several transcendental markers explain the phenomenal vitality of Obama's presidential campaign and its hundreds of thousands of young foot soldiers and Internet contributors. These features also explain why he has been called an "evangelical progressive." I mention (1) the awkward debate on "social-conservative" issues with Ambassador Alan Keyes during the 2004 senate race in Illinois, (2) his formative encounters with certain evangelical Christians and, (3) the influence of M. L. King Jr.'s "Beloved Kingdom."

A DEBATE WITH KEYES

"Christ would not vote for Barack Obama because (he) has voted to behave in a way that is inconceivable for Christ to have behaved" (*The Audacity of Hope*, p. 209).

The doctrinaire and recondite Catholic reactionary was incensed with Obama's magnanimity to all persons, his openness in public policy on gay rights and marriage, and the "last option" of abortion. "Mr. Obama says he's a Christian yet he supports a lifestyle that the Bible calls an abomination . . . He says he's a Christian but he supports the destruction of innocent and sacred life" (p. 209). Seemingly ignoring the truth, the accursing one in the Spirit of God is performing as damnable an act as killing a human person, but Keyes pressed on with his indictment.

Barack Obama was caught short and shocked, perhaps not seeing the absurdity of his accuser. He rejected Keyes's implicit theology and politics, but the ethical point disarmed him. Was there not a shred of truth in the bizarre accusation? The lives of the innocent preborn, like those of the near-dead, were precious and worthy of protection. Family life, and the covenant of life together in raising children, was a salient norm of human existence. He found himself taking some respectful distance from the antipersonalism of the "right to life" school and also from the expediency of the "freedom of choice" school. Even more, he was fathoming the theological and ethical paradox of Kierkegaard, where one held in creative tension the principles of autonomy and advocacy of being. He was becoming a post-liberal evangelical, yet with all of the prophetic ardor that his interlocutor feigned.

EVANGELICAL POLITICS

Part of the Obama phenomenon was a weariness with the Bush/Cheney/Rove co-optation of conservative Christian conscience and betrayal of the allegiance of that community into the reprehensible behaviors as seen in this worldview: exorbitant governmental spending and economic recession, untruth and torture in war ethics, favoritism for the rich and contempt for the poor in Hurricane Katrina, Africa policy, and tax policy. This disenchantment was channeled into interest in Obama by several big name "evangelical" politicos leaving the Christian right in the increasingly strident and embarrassing voices of the likes of Rush Limbaugh and James Dobson. Bill Hybels, Tony Campola, Rick Warren, and T. D. Jakes flirted with the young, unabashedly fervent lawyer-preacher from Chicago—the new epicenter of the evangelical cosmos, Texas having sold its soul.

Evangelical pundits like Ron Seidel and Jim Wallis asked America's broad evangelical constituency to take as seriously the biblical injunctions of racial justice and equity, preferential options for the poor, the rights of women and children, honesty and integrity in public life, international vision and the yearning for peace grounded in justice as it did the conservative imperatives such as abortion and "family (homophobic) values."

These movements in public conviction seemed to account for the wave of primary and caucus support for Obama across the pink states of America, leaving the slivers of blue on East and West Coasts to Hillary.

A moving encounter with a young physician was similarly challenging to Barack. "'I oppose abortion and gay-marriage,' he emailed me. 'I also oppose the idolatry of the free market and the trigger-ready will to attack, invade and occupy in foreign policy,' he continued" (*Audacity of Hope*, 210) Such claims and qualms also sent Barack back to the spiritual/ moral *tabula rasa*.

Surely there was some virtue in free enterprise, right to life, family values, even the much-derided social conservative agenda. How Barack will respond to issues like stem-cell retrieval from aborted embryos, gender specific abortion, Nafta and resistance to free markets, and bombing suspected terrorist havens in places like Pakistan will likely hinge on his emerging theological conviction. We can hope that his maturing consciousness of the thought of Dr. King, Reinhold Niebuhr, Karl Barth, James Cone, Dwight Hopkins, and others will tide him through the onrush of a thousand stump speeches.

Dr. King's beloved community in the last hours of his life will be the surest wisdom I can comment on to his quest. Hoping for a new international justice, respect, and end to the war in Vietnam; struggling for the well-being of poor workers in Memphis; the embodiment of Jesse Jackson's rainbow coalition—where all races, genders, faiths, and nations contend together to resist the blights of war, sickness, environmental destruction, and sectarian strife—this is the animating biblical dream of King's—now Obama's—vision.

At the end of the chapter on "Faith" in *The Audacity of Hope*, Obama returns to his kitchen table in South Side Chicago in a poignant scene reminiscent of Dr. King's Emmaeus-like table fellowship with Coretta one evening in Birmingham. Recorded in his *Stride Toward Freedom*, the day had been terrifying, as had Barack's:

> There are some things that I'm absolutely sure about—the Golden Rule, the need to battle cruelty in all its forms, the value of love and charity, humility and grace. Those beliefs were driven home two years ago when I flew down to Birmingham, Alabama to deliver a speech at the city's Civil Rights Institute. The Institute is right across the street from 16th Street Baptist Church, the site where, in 1963, 4 young children ... lost their lives when a bomb planted by white supremacists exploded during Sunday School ... the young pastor and several deacons showed me the still-visible scar along the wall where the bomb went off. I saw the clock at the back of the church, still frozen at 10:22 am—Sunday school time ... those little girls did not die in vain ... they had awakened the conscience of the nation and helped liberate a people; the bomb had burst a dam to let justice roll down like waters and righteousness like a mighty stream ...
>
> My thoughts turned to my mother and her final days, after cancer had spread through her body and it was clear that there was no coming back ... more than once I ... saw fear flash across her eyes.
>
> I carried such thoughts with me as I left the church ... Late that night, back home in Chicago, I sat at the dinner table, watching Malia and Sasha as they laughed and bickered and resisted their string beans before their mother chased them up the stairs and to their baths. Alone in the kitchen washing the dishes, I imagined my two girls growing up and I felt the ache that every parent must feel ... to snatch up each moment of your child's presence and never let go ... to lock in for all eternity the sight of their curls or the feel of their fingers clasped around yours. I thought of Sasha asking me once what happened when we die—'I don't want to die, Daddy.' I hugged her and said 'You've got a long, long way before you have to worry about that.' ... I wondered whether I should have told her the truth that I wasn't sure what happens when we die, any more than I was sure where the soul resides ... Walking up the stairs I knew what I hoped for—that my mother was together in some way with those four little girls—capable in

some fashion of embracing them, of finding joy in their spirits. I know that there in my daughters that night, I grasped a little bit of heaven. (*The Audacity of Hope*, p. 224–26)

My Comment: Present historical dynamics are, in striking ways, re-enactments of preceding years, persons, and campaigns. Historical events unfold within broad patterns of meaning and value, and their understanding involves deep analysis of the wisdom of sacred literature that is our hermeneutical matrix. It leads me to include the following observations:

"BIBLICAL ABRAHAM AND GLOBAL PEACE AND RECONCILIATION"—NOVEMBER 13, 2012

In reaction to an article by Jon Levenson, "The Idea of Abrahamic Religions: A Qualified Dissent," *Jewish Review of Books*, No. 12 (Winter, 2012).

Jon Levenson has explored in this commentary the difficult issue before the world today as Syria shells The Golan and Israel shells embattled Syria. Meanwhile Free Syria patriots try to coalesce into a unified opposition to the Assad regime and a 30 year old soldier/survivor of the war in Afghanistan writes a book that Tom Wolfe calls a masterpiece "of the grandeur of All Quiet on the Western Front." The book is called *Yellow Birds*. Levenson always gives us sharp biblical theological bearings in biblical religion (which he also seems to believe does not really exist).

This all transpires as the epicenter of our world of terrorism again rears its ugly head—the Israel/Palestine conflict. Again Goliath—Israel has tightened its death bird-cage on Palestine through its occupation, preparing yet another invasion. In suicidal rage Hamas—the chosen government of the Palestinian people and their only social service arm (together with the West Bank Authority in Ramalla)—now rains its tinker-toy rockets on one of the world's most potent military powers—killing a few and terrorizing all as sirens scream and citizens scramble to their bomb shelters. And America—the only power that can mediate the conflict—lets Israel kill ruthlessly with its indefensible violence, destroy again terra sancta—God's home in the world. Meanwhile the Muslim world—including the Arab Spring of renewal-world—disrupts in ineffective rage, and all other nations let the carnage go on with impunity.

Levenson, my Skokie neighbor, sent me a draft of material from his then-forthcoming book, *Inheriting Abraham: The Legacy of the Patriarch in Judaism, Christianity and Islam* (Princeton, 2012). In the personal papers that Levenson provided me, he reflects:

> Confronted with seemingly endless discord in the Middle East—much of it said to be rooted in religious difference—scholars and laymen alike have been promoting the idea of "Abrahamic religion." This is the notion that Judaism, Christianity, and Islam are equally indebted to the figure of Abraham, the patriarch prominent in the Scriptures of all three. Surely, the theory goes, the three communities can move toward much-needed reconciliation by considering their shared origins.
>
> This is a message that the more fanatical members of each community need to hear, but their very fanaticism makes them unlikely to listen. One might also question whether theology, rather than culture and politics, is what lies at the heart of anti-Western and anti-Israeli rhetoric in the Middle East. Commonalities and cross-influences do exist among the three religions, but no less worthy of attention are the differences. . . .
>
> There are three Abrahams, then, not one, and in each religion he is in relationship with a living God who has called a particular community to his service. Instead of attempting to devise some vague pan-Abrahamic religion that elides the actual differences among the three in the name of a bland universalism at odds with their scriptures, we should be wiser to confront the differences honestly and respectfully. The alternative isn't only too easy. It is also false.

My Commentary: In what sense, then, may we look to the conjunction of the three Abrahamic faiths for guidance toward reconciliation and peace among the very three religions which have together—in Holy War, Crusade, and Jihad—fomented so much of war in God's world for thousands of years?

My answer is scriptural reasoning—the practice of reading correlated scriptural texts from the three traditions, e. g., texts about Hannah/Mary in the three traditions often called, in Christianity, the Magnificat. This correlation can then be applied to economic or warfare issues in the present. Contrary to the sense that such trialogue will flame out in a cross fire of anger, it works, well, because of the inescapable affinity of these our faiths in the undergirding "Unicity" of God. "Come let us reason together—says the Lord" (Isa 1:18).

On this point of Abraham and Bible in the contemplation of action in areas of public policy, it would be well to declare my standpoint on the difficult art and act of hermeneutics, which is the discipline of deriving principles and rules for concrete action from sacred or normative texts. In my case, norms come from Holy Scripture, which I see as Jewish and Christian Scriptures corroborated by the derivative midrash on these two literatures in Muslim holy writ (their supplements to the "Book-of the peoples of the book"). My present endeavors in this regard follow the lines in the next chapter.

Twelve

Essay on Interfaith Hermeneutics

Project: Interfaith Hermeneutics: A Study of Paul Ricoeur for Interfaith Work Today.

Purpose: The Project formulates a hermeneutical foundation for interfaith endeavors.

SUCH HERMENEUTICS CONSIDERS BOTH the separable (inherent integrity of each) and the composite kerygma, witness, and message of the three Abrahamic faiths. This author believes in the inherent midrashic and scriptural connection among these three monotheisms to which two-thirds of the world's population ascribe. We find in this faith triad an ongoing scriptural narration. The study of Mary, the mother of Jesus, for example, is the perfect example of the value, indeed, the necessity, of reading Scripture in this way. The Song of Hannah in 1 Samuel 2, the Gospel (Matthew and Luke 1 and 2), and the Quran texts (Surah 5, et al.) constitute a scriptural continuum. Drawing on the life-long labors of Paul Ricoeur, the end-product of the research will be a field guide for programs of interfaith study and action around the world.

The rationale for the project is drawn from an assertion of Hans Kung: "There will be no peace in the world without peace among the religions and there will be no peace among the religions without dialogue among the religions." The urgency of this particular project adds that "there can be no dialogue among the religions without a common language and framework of meaning, interpretation and understanding—a shared hermeneutic." Without such trustful and reciprocal discourse, we will simply continue talking past each other while the fratricidal violence rages on. (See Ken Vaux, *Jew, Christian, Muslim: Faithful Unification or Fateful Trifurcation*, Eugene, OR: Wipf and Stock, 2003.)

Paul Ricoeur, a philosopher, theologian, and Bible scholar, has developed what many consider to be the most useful contemporary hermeneutical system for interpreting Christian existence, especially in its kerygmatic aspect (proclamation). This message, because of its scriptural and philosophical tenor, can readily be entered into interplay with the messages of the fraternal monotheisms of Judaism (Halacha) and Islam (Jihad). My extrapolation and appropriation of Ricoeur's model to the contemporary scene is the groundwork for the following proposal.

Ricoeur is ideally suited to shape and supply this urgently needed project because philosophy has always been the indispensible handmaiden to monotheistic religious theology. Beginning with the antique and classical origins of these cultural enterprises called High Religions (ca. 500 BCE–500 CE), we find Graeco-Roman and Persian philosophy providing interpretive facility to Judaism, Christianity, and Islam in the axis ages of the monotheistic faiths and ethics; Hammurabic ethics and legalities shaping the canons of Israel and Egypt; the theological philosophy of Plato and Plotinus organizing Christianity and Judaism; and Aristotle's metaphysical philosophy weaving its way into Christianity and Islam. At every step, we find philosophy and theology going hand in hand. In the modern age, continental and analytic philosophy, as well as Catholic, Jewish, and Islamic philosophies, continues the same convergence of philosophy and religion in the endeavor of hermeneutics.

Working with the same synthesis of Athens and Jerusalem, Ricoeur characterizes his work as an anthropology of a competent and vulnerable human being. Drawing from the derivative thought of Martha Nussbaum and Amartya Sen, I then amplify Ricoeur's anthropology for our purposes into a theological philosophy of human science comprehending good and evil, hope and despair—an ontological, ecclesial, and political philosophy. I expand his anthropology into a broad spectrum of abilities/disabilities: capabilities, competencies, vulnerabilities, and contemptabilities (wishing to be rid of "others" whom we wish did not exist and whom we undertake to remove from our turf on this good earth). Ricoeur's body of work distributes the seeds for the most hopeful garden that will yield the flourishing fruits for the vital task of interfaith horticulture.

For Ricoeur, humans are inherently able to do justice as the glory of God prompts this grace—*Imago Dei*—within their being. Humans are also fallible in freedom and frailty. The self subsists in space and time (*bios*) and in love/justice and transcendence (*logos*). For the French Reformed lay-theologian, the human is not transparent, whole, and complete—despite his underlying creative freedom and competence—even justice. Following Paul, the apostle, Ambrose, Augustine, Anselm, and Calvin, in concert with philosophical wisdom, human identity resides in the sovereignty of God and is realized in existence in the world in association with other humans (Autre/Autri).

My acquaintance with Ricoeur begins in the 1970s and '80s when we lived in Hyde Park and made sabbaticals in Germany and Paris as Maestro Ricoeur simultaneously taught at the University of Chicago and the Sorbonne. I especially value the times when we were on leave in Strasbourg and belonged to the same church, Saint Pierre, and then in his final years when he was depositing his legacy and archives with fascinating conferences into the Institute Protestante in Paris.

He brought an amazing experience to this vocation. Raised by his grandparents in north-central France in the early years of the First World War, after his mother had died and his father had been killed in the war, he learned hermeneutics and intellectual passion by inculcated biblical study in the families of the Reformed Church. A prisoner in the Second World War in Eastern Europe, he created a prison-university and furthered his intellectual inculcation in the great traditions of existential, phenomenological, and linguistic philosophy. The traditions of Kierkegaard, Saussure, Husserl, Heidegger, and Jaspers; and later Bergson, Derrida, and Levinas would become a salient foundation for his pioneering work in interfaith hermeneutics.

WHAT IS HERMENEUTICS?

A philosopher, Paul Ricoeur, begins with a philosophical understanding of hermeneutics. His system will soon accept amplifications and amendments from theology, anthropology, psychology, sociology, and politics. His beginning definition of hermeneutics would therefore be something like an interpretation of profound issues of meaning and value—life and death, purpose and absurdity—all within the existential and social setting of one's being in the world under God. His work thus begins with the epistemology of thinkers like Heidegger, Husserl, and Gadamer.

Hermeneutics, thus concieved, is obviously a protest against dominant currents of philosophy, both in continental and Anglo-American, analytic traditions. It crosses swords with linguistic analysis, positivism, and deconstruction. Which leads to our second question:

WHAT IS FAITH-TRADITION HERMENEUTICS?

When it comes to the phenomenon of believing—personal conviction and collective faith—hermeneutics involves establishing a mechanism of interpretation of the convictions, practices, assertions, and actions involved in personal and communal identity—vis-à-vis God. This usually involves observing sacred Scriptures, preaching, confessions, language and liturgy, prayer, witness, and testimony—all within a much broader phenomenon of apperceiving the Sacred. To communicate faith(s), educate and inculcate meanings and values, and adjudicate differences and conflicts are cardinal purposes of hermeneutics.

Ricoeur's hermeneutics begin and end with biblical exegesis (language analysis) and exposition (expressed witness) of the faith traditions. They therefore deal with the dimensions derived from Plato and Aristotle (dialectical and ontological), from Paul the apostle, Augustine, Aquinas, Calvin, Kierkegaard, Barth, and Levinas (existential and theistic), where sacred utterance (texts and Midrash) search for an assertion of Being and Being Itself as this *miteinandersein* contours and connects particular being and existence in the world with Being itself.

ETYMOLOGY AND MEANING

As soon as we adjourn to Hermes and hermeneutics, and see the origins of semiotics wherein words become signs or seeds full of potency, we tremble before the awesome possibility of saying truth or falsehood—good or evil. Here we tread on the boundaries of the sacred and divine quarantines. That the divine message and meaning—Logos—has its own terms gives caution to our mimesis (all human thought and act). Ultimately and penultimately, Kierkegaard's Either/Or is all we have in freedom and responsibility.

In theology, this dialectical truth is expressed in the view that human speech is capable of confession or curse. On the great third commandment, we either honor or defame the name of the Holy One. In the great second tablet of Torah, we either serve fellow humanity in care or we harm others in neglect and violence.

Ancient hermeneutics radiating from primal apperception, perception, and articulation (blindness, vision, and speech) is followed in Hellenistic and Hebraic culture by precise semiotics and philosophies of language. After the Homeric bards and Pythagoras, we find Talmudic hermeneutics (beginning Second Temple, ca. 515 BCE) joining the Greek dialectics of truth and ethical skepticism—developing the principles of language and logic (e.g., Hillel's principles of a *forteriori* verification). Christian hermeneutics follows these premises, with apostolic studies of Hebrew Scripture (predictive) and Alexandrian (allegorical) and Antiochean (literal) traditions forwarding elaborate theories of hermeneutical epistemology.

That this human power (or divine gift) exists at the membrane between the secular and the sacred points to a greater truth—formulated most powerfully by Noam Chomsky—that a universal theological/ethical neurology of Spirit makes us accountable beings—knowing right and wrong, comprehension and ignorance, justice and injustice, blindness or vision. Human nature makes us accountable.

WHAT IS INTERFAITH HERMENEUTICS?

Here we see the rationale for interfaith hermeneutics.

Ultimately, matters in the world must be viewed *sub species aeternitatis*.

The whole world—under God or even construed secularly and linguistically universal—is one cosmos of meaning, speech, and justice. This means that nothing less that interfaith hermeneutics can embrace the whole. As we consult Ricoeur and with him, Levinas and Derrida (and the Islamic world he understands and represents in his neoprophetic wisdom), we envision the scope of this universe of discourse. Early Christian rhetoric and hermeneutics in the Second Temple Period (500 BCE —70 CE) sees a convergence among Talmudic, apostolic, and Islamic (Arab poetic) hermeneutics. Literal, allegorical, mystical, and instructional hermeneutics all play a part. This quadrilateral is simply a rendering of semiotic complexification—speech—when true, liberates, moves, convinces, and compels.

In the 1960s, Ricoeur developed in a salient work on Freud and philosophy, the provocative notion that enters the language as the "hermeneutic of suspicion." His long life of faith experience in interfaith cultures and contexts, and in the philosophical idiom, made it clear to him that hermeneutics for today's world must be universal and interfaith in character, and that interfaith reality must of necessity be scriptural (kerygmatical) and hermeneutical.

A biblical dialectic and prophetic impulse comes to characterize his hermeneutics as he joins the double volition of "willingness to suspect and willingness to listen—vowing rigor and vowing obedience" (see *Freud and Philosophy*, New Haven, CT: Yale University Press, 1977, p. 27). He names three new prophets as his "masters of suspicion"—Marx, Nietzsche, and Freud. The logic of indictment is clearly drawn from years of pouring over biblical texts. Smug religion, slavery religion, and delusional religion are roundly condemned. Faith that obsesses on personal salvation at the expense of edification of the community, a slave mentality that arises at the expense of liberation, and pacifying illusions that materialize at the expense of courage and human service, are cast down as idols. One senses the obvious and profound implication of this for interfaith hermeneutics.

CHARACTERISTICS OF AN INTERFAITH HERMENEUTIC

Hermeneutics is marked by a bivalent mood combining iconoclasm and upbuilding—deconstruction and reconstruction. It is a moral enterprise raising technical and material matters to the realm of meaning and value. Hermeneutics is the harbinger of truth and justice in a world that is full of falsehood and injustice. After iconoclasm putting rout to idolatry in the world, and the love/justice ethic dispersing the clouds of neglect and abuse on the human–human and human–world plane, a third characteristic of the hermeneutical transvaluation of values pertains to society.

We are now summoned to the broadest possible realms of association. Hermeneutics tangibly means building bridges, allowing discursive, unitive, and rejuvenating traffic—words and thoughts—to cross impassable chasms of faiths, cultures, animosities, suspicions, even tribal and socio-economic antagonisms and imagined struggles for survival and existence; kill or be killed. Provincialities are surrendered in the processes of speaking and listening as this dispels separation and allows concord, at least, coexistence. Here we have the greatest gift of interfaith hermeneutics.

Outline of This Document

I. Introduction

II. Ricoeur and Interfaith Project: Premises—Guiding Assumptions

III. Ricoeur and the Interfaith Project: Hermeneutical Principles—Truth, Goodness, Justice

IV. Ricoeur and Hermeneutics: Processes of Project—Time Line, Research, and Development of Project

V. Products—Handbook for Field Testing

VI. Programs—Laboratories for Interfaith Endeavors—Europe, Middle East, America, Africa

VII. Conclusion

RICOEUR AND INTERFAITH PROJECT: PREMISES—GUIDING ASSUMPTIONS

At this point, we can see the qualities of a Ricourean hermeneutics that commend it to our consideration as we take up the interfaith task. It becomes a useful instrument for these reasons:

This hermeneutics is a harbinger of proleptic (impending) truth and justice over the prevalent falsehood and evil abroad in the world today. Truth, with its correlate justice, lies in wait to appear in human discourse, waiting for the provocation and evocation of dialogical processes and action endeavors to bring it to the form of thought and word.

A further premise of Ricoeur's hermeneutics is the fragility of the human condition (e.g., fallible man). On this foundation, the human purpose of "caring action" is grounded. Following Heidegger, who intertwines three words: *Dasein* (being there alongside), *Dasein geworfen* (thrown into this precarious being), and *Sorgen* (caregiving), Ricoeur allows that in caring, action words come to life, becoming our habitation of the world and transfiguring threat and danger toward help and efficacy. Like Edith Stein and Dietrich Bonhoeffer, Ricoeur lives out this dangerous judaophilic and Islamophobic existence rather than living the "bad faith" of Professor/Provost Heidegger.

The narrative unity of life occurs within a symphony of other, indeed, all other lives. Narrative, by definition, links the self (the one) into the many (Ricoeur, *Oneself as Another*, Chicago: University of Chicago Press, 1995, p. 163). Story is now joined to memory and tradition (faith history) as well as to ethics and politics—another way of speaking of "living faith" (common trust) and commitment. We begin to see that the simplest assertions of hermeneutics are posited on the basis of a Transcendent/Immanent axis.

Action is therefore about language, i.e., thought transposed into will and expression; rhetoric, which will become action. Hermeneutics, therefore, arises from the rationale of speaking and hearing. Ultimately, this realm of activity is what we call kerygma, message, witness, preaching, proclamation, publication, instruction, and teaching.

Ricoeur's hermeneutics also commends itself by reason of the interfaith world he foresaw and helped bring into being. Toward the end of his life, his archives show that he placed great hope in interfaith conversation and consultation. For sixty years he had been engaged in lively conversation with the Jewish community. Alongside his colleagues and protégées at the University of Strasbourg, with Alsacian magnanimity he supported the development of Jewish and Islamic faculties to complement the established Protestant and Catholic departments. As Institute Catholique became the vehicle for *mullah* preparatory studies in Paris, Ricoeur, who has a lecture room named for him in the halls where Henri de Lubac and Teilhard de Chardin once roamed, supported, and nurtured this development.

This milieu was natural for Ricoeur. France, Germany, and England had already taken on the character of "Eurabia" (Jenkins) with significant Muslim populations building from Algerian/Senegalese, Turkish, and Pakistani immigrations. The discomfort that Jews continue to feel in those once genocidal lands remains a lacunae in the unfolding of interfaith awareness in Europe.

RICOEUR AND THE INTERFAITH PROJECT: HERMENEUTICAL PRINCIPLES— TRUTH, GOODNESS, JUSTICE

Christmas 2011, the same tragic "Silent Night, Holy Night" as last year when bombs in northern Iraq spattered blood on a Malachite Christian cathedral and the neighboring synagogue—now not working. Last night, three churches in Modala, Nigeria, were bombed by Boko Haram, a pro-Shariah terrorist group, and over one hundred lives of worshipers are claimed. —This Haram sect holds that Western laws and ways of life are apostate and dangerous (including Jewish and Christian?). This group claims responsibility.

Meanwhile, as Christians attack Muslims in Jos, Nigeria, America high-tails it out of Iraq after losing ten thousand American lives and perhaps taking 1 million Iraqi lives. Meanwhile, in America's "theater of the absurd" (election year politics), a Christian Right organization in Florida complains that an ad by the retailer Lowe's creates a "false" complementary picture of Muslims—who should, this group argues, be required by law to be pictured as "violent," "Shariah fanatic-mobs."

Into such a morally absurd world, Ricoeur offers three principles for hermeneutical activity: truth, mutual respect, and justice. In the contextual events we review, it is evident that contrary and contradictory narratives and interpretations coexist. Ricoeur, therefore, prefaces the exposition of this tableau with a sketch of the concentric polysemic circles of hermeneutical rhetoric.

A text, first of all, has a surface, literal, simple meaning. Second, a text—written or spoken—has an allegorical or imbedded-meaning. Third, it has a hidden, cryptic, authentic meaning. In the biblical text of Miriam's Song—celebrating God's drowning of the Egyptians as they crossed the sea in pursuit of the Hebrew people—we have voice one and two (Genesis Rabah), vindictive glee at the judgment. Then God's voice is heard: "What are you celebrating—they, too, are my people." Such nuance marks mature and authentic reading of religious texts.

Truth

The matrix of three principles is ancient. To the Greeks' freedom, beneficence, and justice is added Christianity's faith, hope, and charity. Classical and Christian civilization juxtapose virtues and vices, graces and sins.

Modern philosophical ethics has settled on a shorthand mantra—autonomy, nonmaleficence/beneficence and justice—sweeping under the rug the mischievous fact that these virtues andvices can be ethically substantive or simply formal processes. Freedom can be the deepest and most precious quality—without which we could not bear to live—or a banal, even dangerous "do your own thing" anomie.

Truth can entail both formidable and all-surpassing absolutism as well as the crudest Machiavellian relativism. Anchored in Hebraic, Hellenic, and Christian history, it becomes the sine qua non of all human interchange. A glance at the valences of the *truth/untruth—veracity/mendacity* axes reveals the rich and sublime dimensions as well as the mundane and pervasive trickery involved within this range of human conception, deliberation, and action.

The procedural nature of truth-telling usually invokes criterion such as correspondence (appearance and reality), coherence and consistency (internal corroboration), and other features of rational compulsion.

Substantively, and attending to agency, attention is called to a broad spectrum of kinds and gradations of truth and falsehood ranging on the truth side from killing objectivity to liberating silence, and on the falsehood continuum from quixotic delusion to flattery to the "little white lie."

To illustrate the relevance of "truth" to hermeneutical principles, I cite (now former) Chinese president Hu Jintao in an essay circulated in early 2012. In a magazine going back to Mao Zedong entitled *Seeking Truth* (see Edward Wong, *New York Times*, Jan. 4, 2012, A7), the president decries the "spiritual and cultural vacuum in China which is now being filled by 'spiritual and cultural (including moral)' corruptions from the West being foisted by America in materialism and imperialism, commercialism and sensualism, injustice and violence—in order to divide and destroy the Chinese people." (They should talk!—my comment.)

The supreme irony of this critique is that China herself is exporting throughout the world the same catalogue of vices, all the while suppressing the antidotes of those same evils through human rights violations and abrogation of freedom, as well as suppression of freedom of religion—Christianity, both Catholic and evangelical; vibrant Islam in the provinces; and Buddhism in Tibet. Interfaith vitality and hermeneutics of truth remain the best guard against the "lie"—the harbinger of liberating "truth."

Freedom is the concomitant of truth and truth is the indispensible foundation for the procession of truth—freedom of inquiry, of expression, of association, of work, of faith, of life itself. Let us now see how Ricoeur defines and delineates this cardinal value.

In our confused and ethically/spiritually bewildered world, we are not able to comprehend freedom or bondage. We confuse freedom with free enterprise or freedom to "do our own thing." Like Luther, we often confuse bondage with certitude and safety. Risk and exposure may be a better freedom. We do well to recapture his deeper synthesis—rising from his dialogue with Erasmus: "The Christian is the perfectly free Lord of all, subject to none and the perfectly bound servant of all, subject to all." License, per se, is not liberty. Genuine love and service—concern and care for l'autre—is. When Pilate queried Jesus—"what is *truth*?"—truth stood right before him and he didn't see. In the truth, we are emboldened to speak truth to power rather than shrink into silence.

Ricoeur has specifically grappled with the theme of truth—so rudimentary to philosophy with its canons of logic, epistemology, and metaphysics; and theology with its canons of divinity, incarnation, prophesy, and word. He offers this in his discussions of history and truth, his dialogues with Gadamer on Truth and Method (*Wahrheit und Methode*) and in his vast interstitial writing and speaking on memory, history, and oblivion—(*La Mémoire, l'histoire et l'oubli*).

Throughout his writing, teaching, and religious instruction, he has been asking how we can represent the past (and present) with accuracy, fidelity, and trust. How can something past, archaic and historic matters, be represented so that they are credible and worthy of transmission? In the deep corridors of meaning—dealings of the Gods with humanity in mythic events, historical records, reported comings, theophanies, epiphanies, and verbal receipts (prophesies, wisdom, Torah, psalms, apocalypses, gospels, Epistles)—how can we convey these sacred trusts with truth, (i.e, with the authority of the giver and source of all truth. To say *gegraptai* (it stands written) is to stand on pure Word—Verbum Dei—Truth, per se. We are creatures—parents, neighbors, pastors, beings—who can, and therefore must, remember, articulate, transmit, talk, write, recollect, discard erroneous accretions and ammendations. We live out and stake our lives on what we say, testify to, witness about, and live by.

Goodness (Righteousness)

The second archaic and universal, biblical and philosophical principle to ground and guide hermeneutics is the familiar axis of eschewing evil and doing good. Derived from theological and rational wisdom, this principle extols the virtue of doubt, suspended belief, and iconoclasm on the one hand; and active commitment and action on the other. Adhering to the first maxim of true religion, "no false gods," contends that the first duty of beneficence is nonmaleficence—Hippocrites's "first of all, do no harm." Thought, will, language, and action that proceeds from interpretive action (hermeneutics) is in the first case the "hermeneutics of suspicion."

But deconstruction is not the end and purpose of human discernment seeking to be responsible. We must cast down idols in order to execute righteousness or goodness but not slip into the black hole of unending skepticism and cynicism. Construction and edification of others and the world is the task of doing good.

Ricoeur was steeped in the Jewish and Christian ethic of love of God and neighbor. He had learned this from a cultural experience sullied by a deep anti-Semitism that he always resisted. At the end of his life, he was also undergoing the transition into late modernity by becoming aware of the traditions of Islam, both in the universities of Paris and Chicago, and from his Parisienne colleagues of Semitic culture and persuasion such as Emmanuel Levinas and Jacques Derrida. My research at Fonds Ricoeur shows clearly—especially in his later activities and diary entries—that he was moving in an interfaith direction. Throughout Europe, Africa, and America, his salient work was beginning to be seen as an instrument of guidance—especially guidance into scriptural hermeneutics—for our arising interfaith world.

Caring in Truth

In his encyclical, "Caritas in Veritate," Pope Benedict XVI wrote that gratuity—kindness extended in love without requirement for recognition or reward—is necessary for the economic well being of people and the world. In our mean-spirited, pecuniary world—where 1 percent of the population controls 39 percent of the world's wealth (and half of those 1 percent live in America)—this strikes us as a strange and peculiarly idealistic utopian dream. Indeed, there seems today to be a frantic clinging to this ill-begotten wealth, using liberty from taxation to retain privilege by "buying elections" (cf. Iowa Caucuses) and "guiding government process" by irresistible lobbying by vested interests.

It is very likely that the philosopher-pope not only follows the ancient magisterial tradition of teaching about the poor but also the work of Paul Ricoeur. Ricoeur wrote that in the gospel "the logic of generosity clashes head on with the logic of equivalence which orders everyday exchanges, commerce and our penal law" ("America: The National Catholic Review," Aug. 3, 2009). Generosity (benevolence generating beneficence) is the heartland of a caritas (interfaith) ethic—always at variance with the commercial ethic that at best demands recompense and at worse gouges the meager resources of the poor so that those who have little now have even less.

Ricoeur argues that kindness, mercy, and benevolence are ontological—i.e., it pertains to being itself and the very "ground of being" (Tillich). It is not a philanthropic gift but a give-back since everything we are and have is not ours. Present political rhetoric vociferously proclaiming that "what we have belongs to us" is especially odious and false—despite the cheers it elicits. Sharing out of "common-wealth" ethic—a Koinonia ethic is a ground-work teaching that Ricoeur learned from his faith tradition teacher, Jean Calvin, where the well-being of each requires the well-being of all and all are blessed in teaching of Calvin, Andre Bieler, and Ernst Fuchs—"La Mystere des pauvres et des riches."

As I write this material, I listen to the Vienna Philharmonic playing Gustav Mahler's Fourth Symphony, "Das himmlische Leben."

Kathleen Battle sings the final movement:

> We enjoy heavenly pleasures and leave the earth behind
> No worldly tumult is heard in heaven;
> All live in gentlest peace, In gentlest peace.

Ricoeur accesses this worldly provision and ethical imperative not as "pie in the sky"—remember, Marx is one of the saints of his hermeneutic of suspicion. This is a real-world heritage in the provision of a gracious God and his preferential option for the poor. It is the expected life-response of those whose endowments entail what it takes to feed the poor, heal the sick, and release the prisoners. Gifts commensurate to needs are profuse in the earth and unless hoarded or stolen, they are distributed as intended.

Secular bioethics and legal and economic ethics have adopted the Kennedy mantra to classify and analyze ethics decisions in nonreligious terms, though still resonant with those deeper normative-ethical traditions, such as are found in Judaism, Christianity, and Islam. Even Hinduism, Confucianism, Buddhism, and Secular Humanism can recognize and utilize this nomenclature and hermeneutics. *Freedom, beneficence*, and *justice* have achieved such currency. Such secular derivatives of deeper wellsprings of value may accord with a hermeneutics of those deeper belief structures.

Justice

Ricoeur's system of thought, belief, and value focuses ultimately on *justice*. In his later years, he was working intensely on the theme of justice and on the nature of the just person and a just society. The writings at his life's end (ca. 2005) focus on the tension between love and justice (see W. David Hall, *Paul Ricoeur and the Poetic Imagination*, New York: SUNY Press, 2008). This antinomy is not new. Indeed, for forty years, this tension has characterized the field of Anglo-American "religious ethics"— with pioneer thinkers like the Niebuhr brothers, Joseph Fletcher and Paul Ramsey, Richard McCormick, and others. Some ask whether love can pertain to structures—corporations and governments—or only justice.

Ricoeur takes a comingled ethical heritage to a greater depth. In transcending his own continental heritage (existential, phenomenological—Heidegger, Hegel, Husserl, and hermeneutical), he takes our reflection to new levels of possibility. In transcending the Anglo-American heritage he learned in Chicago, he brings that school of thought to new depths. Here, in America, he not only conjoins analytic (linguistic) and Continental (French and German) traditions of the hermeneutics of language, but he joins his Eurocentric Islamophilia with the Judaeophilia more culturally embedded in the American ethos. As a European/American hybrid, he has become an interfaith devotee. My task in this project is to sketch out the road maps of this new adventure from this GPS. What are the directions from this map?

With his associate, Emmanuel Levinas, Ricoeur is always exploring Judaic and Rabbinic materials. Biblical texts, in their hermeneutical depth and power, take center stage in this epistemology, which is not a particularly strong penchant in American thought. As Hall shows, we are now dealing in Ricoeur with poetics: phenomenology, psychology, the arts, politics, and society. These are complemented by the American emphases of language analysis and philosophical positivism.

In his book, *Reflections on the Just* (Chicago: University of Chicago Press, 2000), Ricoeur delineates his meditation on public theology, policy, and law. He now deals with jurisprudence and forensic theology: judging, accusing, examining, weighing evidence, arguing, sentencing, pardoning, and a raft of cognate issues. He is here developing a fresh treatment of the issues of a philosophy of law: Aristotle, Kant, Arendt, Rawls, Walzer are all invoked along with theogical voices, such as Hebrew and Christian casuistic texts—e.g., the Sermon on the Mount—Paul and Augustine, Islamic theocentric law, Aquinas and Calvin, Barth and neotheological social philosophies: Levinas, Derrida, Regina Schwartz, and many others.

Ricoeur's ethics of justice is unique and creative of a new discourse—both sacred and secular because it utilizes but also redefines and transcends the canons of philosophy (teleology, deontology, and utility) as well as those of theology (command, Logos, word of God, textual authority, and community wisdom). He invites us to explore a new dialogical, hermeneutical, and interfaith consciousness that accents human competencies, integrities, and associations. We end up with an invigorated hermeneutics of knowledge and action that is personal and interpersonal, damning and liberating.

The resulting hermeneutic is perfectly suited for interfaith work. It has the flavor of Jeremiah and the prophets (e.g., fracturing and repairing the created human vessel: Paul, the apostle; e.g., Corinthian correspondence; Augustine's Sermons; Pascal's Meditations; Kierkegaard, the reflections on Torah, prophets, and gospel narratives; e.g., fear and trembling: Abraham/Issac; and Sickness Unto Death: Lazarus, Jesus. The narratives of normativity and vitality (life-events) now become the themes of hermeneutics.

Ricoeur puts it this way: From the suffering other comes a gift that is not from the abstractions of reason, existence, being, or conscience but is from the "weakness itself" (*Oneself as Another*, Chicago: University of Chicago Press, 1995, pp. 188, 189; and J. Moltmann in *The Crucified God*, Minneapolis: Fortress, 1993). For Ricoeur the vulnerable possess and portray power, the sick fathom well-being and health, the dying live into the mystery of resurrection and hope (think of the Eighth Symphony of Gustav Mahler with the concluding movement on "Das Himmlische

Leben.") In life's extremis, we touch the fullness of life. Justice is rightly perceived only in this eschatological horizon.

Justice and Eschatology: The Case of Pardon

The interfaith horizon supplies the place for such eschatological awareness. Ricoeur ponders this mystery of good and evil in a debate on the theme of pardon, vis-a-vis the Holocaust, with a Hungarian philosopher—Sorin Antohi. The question at stake is of the most fundamental in the realms of human social interaction, the broad and deep patterns of history, and the interaction of tribes, nations, and faiths. Justice ultimately devolves toward two poles, revenge or punishment (restoration)—justice or love.

In intertwining anthropocentric and theocentric ways of viewing human affairs, Antohi and Ricoeur explore the thorny question of asking for forgiveness. Here is the difficulty. One who has raped and killed one's neighbor's family in the Hutu/Tutsi conflict in Rwanda or dehumanized black neighbors through apartheid in Mandela's South Africa poses a vastly different question from that requested by the bishops of the European Roman Catholic Church, asking for the families of those killed in the Holocaust for forgiveness from the complicity of the church in that horror.

Ricoeur, after Hegel, believes that punishment—unless redeemed—always entails the repetition of vengeance. Therefore, justice must be humanized. The quality of mercy transfigures justice into true justice, which is recognition, repentance, and redemption. The French use the cognate words—amnesia and amnesty—to talk about a false consciousness that strips justice of its deeper truth.

Ricoeur then ruminates on the long arch of history. In European history, we think of the Turks and the Spanish in early modern atrocities; or the Protestant and Catholic wars of religion; or the Germans, Poles, and French with the Jews in recent history. America, likewise, joined the genocide history, adding judaocide and sinocide to its historic cleansing of the Amerindians in its concentration policies and explicit exterminations, as well as its treatment of Africans in the "Great Passage." As I write, the State of North Carolina has agreed to compensate with $50,000 recompense the few survivors left from the sterilization debacle of the 1930s through the 1950s of black Americans. In another unspeakable desecration of the magnitude of Abu Ghraib, American soldiers are filmed urinating on the bodies of dead Muslim fighters in Afghanistan. Forgiveness involves recognizing, making account, and offering recompense. Love is the touchstone of justice as mercy is the transformation of anger and rage into good will. To live on is not to forget but to pardon.

RICOEUR AND HERMENEUTICS: PROCESSES OF PROJECT—TIME LINE, RESEARCH, AND DEVELOPMENT OF PROJECT

Invasions and occupations of Iraq and Afghanistan, ten years of war and thousands of coalition lives and hundreds of thousands of indigenous lives—and now, perhaps, trillions of dollars in treasure—have been lost because four Marines expressed their rage for their buddies killed in what was conceived by both sides as a "Holy War" protecting and securing homelands by consecrated warriors (U.S. Marines on the one hand and Taliban "Freedom Fighters" on the other). What a world! The context of this fiasco points to the dangerous and ominous depths of our interfaith times, personal and public, secular and sacred issues.

An accurate GPS on this geography of contemporary history and human experience shows that a careful and efficacious hermeneutics requires a set of processes to guide our journey through this jagged terrain. What was called in Enlightenment scriptural study *Sitz im Leben* (life-context) involves discerning a narrative in its originating situation so that we can then use hermeneutical methods to appropriate that message into a contemporary setting.

Having already laid out the principles of the hermeneutical process and the underlying assumptive premises, we can now lay out operational processes that we will call on to bring about the purposes we envision. Here I am simply drawing a sketch of activities that will be called on to assess the value of a Ricoeur mode of hermeneutics in interfaith endeavors. From this laboratory, we will assemble a guidebook for the use of the many persons and groups around the world who are attempting to bring about interfaith dialogue, understanding, and peace. This section will build on two previous books in which I sought to sketch the intellectual and practical landscapes of interfaith exploration and collaboration: *Jew, Christian and Muslim: Faithful Unification of Fateful Trifurcation?: Word, Way, Worship and War in the Abrahamic Faiths* and *Journey Into an Interfaith World: Jews, Christians, and Muslims in a World Come of Age* (Ken Vaux, Eugene, OR: Wipf and Stock, 2003 and 2010).

Hermeneutics is an activity of mining or dredging—hauling up treasure from the deep. It is a set of processes involving retrieving, recovering, and then building foundations. To undertake such maneuvers, careful geological and topographical mapping must first be undertaken. Without such careful location and subterranean and suboceanic description, we can never expect to hit "pay dirt," find oil or gas, and refine and fuel our cars and homes. Without such careful retrieval, there is no Thanksgiving—planes, trains, cars, busses, and L-trains.

Hermeneutics, in this analogy, is gold-mining. It involves identifying and discarding dross ore, finding the commonly desirable *echte Mineral*, gathering, refining, and justly distributing the sustaining substance—gold, coal, oil, gas, harvests, wells, and springs—to all who need this common heritage. Here we remember that "the earth and the sub-earth, the waters and rains, snow and skies belong to 'the Lord'" (Genesis, Isaiah, Job), not to individuals, nations, corporations, or the other seizures and control-grabs to which our finite laws, rules, customs, ownerships, and trespasses lay claim to commonwealth.

In early 2012, we find ourselves at the 150th anniversary of the discovery of oil in Pennsylvania—Oil City, Titusville, Pithole. The substantial resources were extracted and gone in a few short years. Now, it is the vast Marcellus shale deposit that contains a treasure of embedded natural gas which holds some promise of relieving this nation of its dangerous reliance to Middle East and African oil and of rejuvenating the impoverished communities of Appalachia. The treasure lies under Oil City, Pennsylvania; Morgantown, West Virginia; Steubenville, Ohio, and Newburgh, New York—all economically depressed areas.

To get this gas involves dealing with aggressive and greedy corporations, opportunistic lawyers and law suits, land abusing and stream and river-despoiling drilling, and fracking (chemical extraction miles deep under the pristine forests), and maybe jobs for high unemployment areas—but maybe a fly-by-night rapid extraction with a few taking all the rewards and the area rapidly returning to endemic poverty.

And so with the deep springs of our spiritual and ethical resources, what processes are needed for this retrieval and recovery?

The subterranean and subliminal (subconscious) resources calling for the hermeneutical probe and presentation are worldwide and generously universal in their deposit. They also reside in certain places and provinces of faith tradition deposit. My own preliminary probes in a fifty year exploratory career have proceeded from Chicago and America to Britain and Europe, then to Africa and the Middle East. Here at the source grounds of the faiths of Abraham (Israel, Palestine, Egypt, Syria, Lebanon, Armenia, and Turkey) and then in Greece, Italy, Spain, France, Germany, Belgium, Holland, and Britain from which came the Eurocentric founders of America. The full circle of Ken Vaux.

It is in these precincts, admittedly a selective portion of the great global panorama of world religion, that the hermeneutics project will begin. I will survey this terrain and subterrain after a brief proviso.

In his new book, Robert Bellah, (*Religion in Human Evolution*, Cambridge, MA: Harvard University Press, 2011) perhaps the most eminent sociologist of religion in the West, claims that the evolutionary process must acknowledge four primary springs of religious consciousness—if we focus on the axis-place and axis-time (ca. 500 BCE–Present) of the majority of peoples of monotheistic belief. The four are somewhat surprising: Ancient Israel, Classical Greece, Indian Buddhism, and Chinese Confucianism. Where are Christianity and Islam, the fastest growing faith traditions in the world, at present? Perhaps subsumed into Judaism? Perhaps these two dynamic and tension-filled traditions will not ultimately succeed in the wide and long history of human evolution because of their inherent violence? Only time (and space) will tell.

This geocentric and evolutionary history is the setting for our stories, our beliefs and values, and we must begin here. Here our inherited visions of time and eternity, of humanity and divinity, of good and evil, meaning and absurdity, are grounded—perhaps in both senses of that word.

PROGRAMS—LABORATORIES FOR INTERFAITH ENDEAVORS—EUROPE, MIDDLE EAST, AMERICA, AFRICA

The process will follow this pattern: After the manual, questionnaire, and guidelines are published—written and electronic—the following network can serve as a laboratory to field-test the concepts and implementation.

Chicago Soundings: Interfaith activities at Garrett Seminary, Northwestern University, other area universities and seminaries, Evanston congregations, Chicago religious associations, and the Parliament of World Religions.

U.S.A. Centers: Yale, Harvard, Princeton, Virginia, Scriptural Reasoning centers, Centers of Jewish, Christian, and Muslim studies.

Britain: Cambridge University, London: St. Ethelburga's Church and Center.

Paris: Paul Ricoeur Research Center, Institute Protestante and Institute Catholique, American Church and circle of L'Eglise Réformée, Jewish, Islamic, and African Studies in the Sorbonne, Solo dei Gloriam.

To summarize the process envisioned, recall the passage from the brilliant family biography *A River Runs Through It* (Chicago: University of Chicago Press, 1989) where fly-fishing on the surging streams of Montana offers the exquisite metaphor of world, the water-world, a deep, subterranean and sacred world, in these words: "and under the water was the rocks and under the rocks was the Word." This is the delving and discovering process of hermeneutics.

In the process of soundings, mapped above, the project will take the drafted guide—the substantive background paper, research questionnaire, and implementation guidelines and use it throughout the places just listed as a laboratory—with the help of instruments like the SR parallels of cognate texts from the Hebrew Bible, the New Testament, and the Quran; and the new parallel publications of the Torah, the New Testament, and Quran—finally evaluating the project by assessing the helpfulness of Ricoeur's hermeneutics, the interactive guidelines, and the outcomes in changed attitudes and behaviors at the interfaith level in various cultures.

CONCLUSION

Today (January 18, 2012) is the World Day of Prayer for Christian Unity. In Chicago, we celebrate this event on the eve of the Dr. Martin Luther King Jr. holiday. Christian unity is the first and prerequisite step to the unity of the human family and the "unity," the "oneness" of the one God of the whole world. It is therefore fundamental to faith-hermeneutics.

My mentor in this area is the long-time Anglican Bishop of Cairo and Oxford professor, Kenneth Cragg. Basing his arguments on 1 Corinthians and Paul's stringent rebuke of the "dividers" of the fellowship who claimed "I am of Paul, I belong to Apollos, I'm in Christ (not you)," God forbid, Paul admonishes, that we lose our bearings in and on truth. We are to "be one in Christ—you are Christ's and Christ is God's" (1 Cor 3:23). We are Russian dolls of belonging within and without one another, and to cut ourselves off from God, Jesus the mediator, and one another is nothing less than suicide and deicide.

The argument has two parts: (1) God is in Christ/Christ is in God and (2) God is "with us—God is Emmanuel in many and wondrous ways" (*Christ and the Faiths*, Louisville, KY: Westminster John Knox, 1987, p. 175). This expansive Christology and theology accords with what I have discovered in fifty years of ministry in the field of biblical hermeneutics and interfaith studies.

The course of processes will seek to probe this fundamental interfaith point. In past years, we have developed the needed experts, contacts, working groups, and cooperating institutions and these colleagues around the world now stand by to test our hypotheses and operative suggestions.

In my fundamental work—ethics and the Gulf War, ethics and the War of/on Terrorism, Jew, Christian, Muslim, Journey into an Interfaith World—I offer a template which has been forged in the warm coals of Ken Cragg's thought. I am looking to test the viability of a more expansive view of Christ. In Paul's terms, we must not trivialize or miniaturize Christ. We must not even extol our construal of Christ as being inclusive to us, thereby excluding the other peoples of the world and all other stories of God with us—which in the end is what Christology is all about. God is the Triune God—the Living God—the One God of all creation, Emmanuel. This is the hypothesis that Interfaith Hermeneutics seeks to establish.

Thirteen

Aftermath of the Election
War, Sexuality, Interfaith Events

Veteran's Day—November 11–13, 2012.

Now Israel and Gaza launch rockets at each other, ground war is threatened, and meanwhile the country either exults or laments clusters of issues, which revolve around sex and war. Four states have done something about marriage equality, rights for gay and lesbian persons; the election results soundly repudiated the frightful games of controlling the sexual matters and the bodily choices of women in rape (legitimate, divinely chosen, whatever), contraception, gay rights, and other related matters. Flirting with libertarianism, autonomy, interpersonal responsibility or governmental control, fear and hope abounded. Young people have grown up in crucibles of diversity—all races and colors, gays and straights, rich and poor, male female and LGBTs—and they have learned a sublime tolerance. Their counterparts—angry old white men tried to hold on to the ancient regime of privilege and power.

Then sexuality came to intertwine with matters of war. Shakespeare and other writers of all of the world's great literature present the tragic interplay of making love, war, and lying. Now two distinguished military leaders have been implicated in scandals of infidelity. This breaking trust perhaps touched the high-power zones of subversion, blackmail, and the very security of the nation. A troubling question presents itself as we reflect back on General Dwight Eisenhower, and we wonder whether moral turpitude is concomitant with military courage. I often wonder whether Plato struggles with this perplexing matter in *The Republic*. Beyond that conjecture in this age of e-mails, Twitter, and Facebook—everything and everyone is totally transparent to every other. Integrity and privacy have disappeared from the face of the earth. Honesty, integrity, and purity are not only self-affirmed and inculcated in home, school, and church but now buttressed (or brutalized) by public scrutiny, this may mute or foster the frightful dictum that it is not what you will and do but what you are caught thinking and doing.

And the election was about this. Wars are winding down, hopefully not to erupt again—at least not too quickly. Wars, military budgets, and wealth concentration in the hands of the few have brought this nation and many others to their knees. Could freedom and humanity—human opportunity, work, and shared prosperity be shared more equitably around the world? America and Europe, the Arab Spring, and Africa, now on the precipice of calamity, with the spectre of disease and poverty robbing whole nations of any prospect of human fulfillment. Freud thought that all meaning boiled down to love and work. In his debate with C. S. Lewis, the atheist and true believer found common ground. In a time such as this, we may be getting to some "holy ground."

THANKSGIVING, GIFTS, AND "SACRO-WORLDLY" HERMENEUTICS: MID AND LATE NOVEMBER, 2012

This is a tedious chronos punctuated by disruptive/liberative *kairos*. Indeed, the moment seems to be threatened by chaos. Threatening words like "fiscal cliff," "double dip recession," and "Armageddon on the Israeli/Gaza Plain" are all around. Meanwhile, neighbors in my hometown of Hempstead, New York, still lack power from Superstorm Sandy and my family members wait for the next shoe to drop. Worldly events, in other words, assume "biblical" proportion. The time has come for hermeneutical correlation to see what historical events mean in the divine cosmology and economy.

Here is how the hermeneutical process goes: In the scriptural world we meet the "history of God." This God is the God of all the world. This world is enraptured in a redemptive, justice-delivering process. This encounter of God and people is spoken of in terms of God's ear for, care for, and power—wielding regard for the poor, the weak, the sick, and the old. In my teaching, I call this a transaction between the book of life and the tree of life.

The arc of scriptural story is "God's preferential option for the poor." This scriptural revelation is the sine qua non for human political action to bring about those goods and warning earth's peoples to stop visiting injustice and exploitation on the weak. Which brings us back to crises in the world, wars, elections, economics, and international relations. This sketch is the hermeneutical circle beginning with "hermeneutical suspicion" and consummating in ethical action.

In the first press conference of his second term, President Obama declared himself a staunch defender and advocate of the "middle class." I was troubled by this assertion. There was something unseemly in this accent. The Bible does not cry out "blessed is the middle class—they are the kingdom of God." I would have preferred that he had said "I am president of all people in this country." "Democrats and Republicans, middle, upper, and lower classes—gays and straights, youth and elders, rich and poor—red states and blue states and purple states—we are all the American people."

If the truth be known about his mandate, Barack was elected by the poor and lower classes of this nation: inner-city blacks and Hispanics. His great majorities came from those making less than $30,000 dollars a year, less than $50,000 dollars a year. He got a lot of the "working people" (whatever that means), but the rightly called middle class, upper-middle class, and the great majority of wealthier persons in this country not only voted for Romney, they voted against Obama.

Later footnote: CNN reported today (November 21) that "lower-middle class worker citizens will absorb most of the pain if we go "over the financial cliff." If we keep tax cuts for all who make less than $250,000 dollars, those making less than $30,000 dollars, instead of gaining $150 dollars, will now pay $1,450 dollars per year.

Obama's slender majority, 3-plus million in the popular vote, 51% to 49%, a 332–206 electoral college win, was a patchwork, hodge-podge of minority groups: 18% were blacks, 12% were Hispanics, 12% were gays, straights, and bisexuals, 15% were youth, 15% were single women, and the remainder of his 100% were a representative slice of the total electorate. In striking contrast to the general red of the whole country are the blue slivers of West Coast, East Coast, and the upper Midwest, with deep blue toning in the cities of Los Angeles, San Francisco, Phoenix, Dallas, Houston, Atlanta, Chicago, Cleveland, Philadelphia, New York, Boston,

Washington, D.C., and even deeper Democratic concentration in the blighted cores of those cities. Obama's base is dirt poor.

Noting these demographics, candidate Romney said that he lost the election because the president promised these constituencies "gifts" from the government—Dream Act citizenship for Hispanics, more Row v. Wade allowances for abortion and Planned Parenthood provision of contraception for women, reduced student-loan costs for students, continued Social Security and Medicare for seniors like myself, marriage equality for gays and lesbians—etc, etc. These "gifts," he might have added, were he not such a persona non grata with the Republicans, were much sweeter candy than the gifts of austerity, smaller government, and tax cuts for the rich promised by Romney.

Again, if I were writing this speech for Barack Obama, I would have said, "I am the president of all the people in this land—rich and poor, middle, upper, or lower class, white and black, male and female, gay and straight, friend and enemy, whether you voted for me or not."

My Thanksgiving thoughts: "Gifts" are freely given with no expectations of return. Remember the praise song "Give Thanks"—one of the few I can get into.

Hermeneutical reasoning knows that weak and strong and rich and poor antinomies are bridges between biblical and political realities. The greatest biblical chant on thanksgiving is "Thanks Be to Thee" (Handel). The best known popular hymn throughout Christendom might be:

Nun danket alle Gott: Now thank we all our God, (1635, Martin Rinkart).

> Now thank we all our God, with heart and hands and voices,
> Who wondrous things has done, in Whom this world rejoices;
> Who from our mothers' arms has blessed us on our way
> With countless gifts of love, and still is ours today.
>
> O may this bounteous God through all our life be near us,
> With ever joyful hearts and blessed peace to cheer us;
> And keep us still in His grace, and guide us when perplexed;
> And free us from all ills, in this world and the next!
>
> All praise and thanks to God the Father now be given;
> The Son and Him Who reigns with Them in highest Heaven;
> The one eternal God, whom earth and Heaven adore;
> For thus it was, is now, and shall be evermore.

In interfaith theology, "all good and perfect gifts come from above—from the Father of Lights" (James 1:17). Gifts and thanksgiving is anchored in this transcendental frame of reference. One "who from our mother's arms (and into the arms of death and beyond) has blessed us on our way, with countless gifts of love . . ." This great song tells us of one who is bounteous to all, who wills that equality prevail among us with that bounty and that none should have "too much" and none "too little" (2 Cor 8, 9) but that all shall have sufficient daily bread, which is tomorrow's meat.

Thanksgiving is exemplified in autumn harvest festivals; in Passover celebrations of sharing and "Day of Atonement" recollections of life-past gratitude and life-coming hope as proven past and presumed future providence is extolled . . . as it was, is now and ever will be; in thanks for being led, across the sea; in Pilgrim Thanksgiving and old European Christmas; in the Muslim Id al-Adha—everywhere and in every time gifts are exchanged, the poor are remembered and the Giver of All is honored with our gratitude and generosity.

NOVEMBER 20, 2012—INTERFAITH ASPECTS OF INTERNATIONAL EVENTS

Gaza is a pile of rubble. An innocent family of eight has been killed and their home reduced to ashes. More lives lost and more destruction than all harm done to Israel through all the tinker-toy rockets. History repeats itself. It seems that this same scenario floods our helpless consciousness every few years. Secretary of State Hillary Clinton heads for Jerusalem and Ramallah and Cairo while John McCain grumbles away in his deep bitterness at United Nations Ambassador Susan Rice and President Obama.

Still in Cambodia and Myanmar, Obama encourages Burma and its fifty-year-old military government to quell political and ethnic strife. Buddhists savagely kill Muslims in the north. And as the president celebrates at a Buddha shrine and asks a monk to pray for his upcoming budget negotiations, we recall that Muslims seem to love to demolish Buddhist holy sites (e.g., Mali). Meanwhile, in Gaza/Israel, Jews and Muslims seem locked in the fatal embrace that has gone on forever.

THANKSGIVING SUNDAY, NOV 25, 2012

Pastor Ray's Scripture selection of 1 Tim 2: 1-8 seems providential and problematic:

> First of all, then, I urge that supplications, prayers, intercessions, and thanksgivings be made for everyone, for kings and all who are in high positions, so that we may lead a quiet and peaceable life in all godliness and dignity,

> This is right and is acceptable in the sight of God our Savior, who desires everyone to be saved and to come to the knowledge of the truth,

> For there is one God; there is also one mediator between God and humankind, Christ Jesus, himself human, who gave himself a ransom for all—this was attested at the right time,

> For this I was appointed a herald and an apostle (I am telling the truth, I am not lying), a teacher of the Gentiles in faith and truth, I desire, then, that in every place the men should pray, lifting up holy hands without anger or argument.

There it is again, that troubling commission that has hounded my existence for sixty years: "I was appointed a herald [Karux], and an apostle [Apostelos] and teacher to the nations [*Didaskolos Ethnon*]" (1 Tim 2:11). And the even more intimidating surrounding notions, "I therefore speak truth not lie [*aletheia* not *pseudomai*]" and then... a teacher "in faith and truth." The admonition of James follows immediately—therefore, "not many of you ought to become teachers..."

Teaching to the nations is a command (mitzvot) that haunts me. I watch the world at the brink this early morning from ancient Gaza—and no one will speak and no one tells the truth. We will not tolerate truth just as we would not in the political campaign we have been chronicling: "they (Israel) started it"—"no, they (the Palestinians) started it, and we will finish it."

Then some guy named Morsi—a Muslim Brother like Hamas, the elected government of Gaza—declares himself King and Lord (a new Napoleon, who called himself "the state"). And then like Pharaohs of old, "by the will of God and the people's ballot," he declares himself the sacred King and directs the people to pray for him. The newly democratic Jasmine Revolution throng demonstrates their will in Tahrir Square, and the military looks on. Our crazy, wonderful world.

Gaza (Hamas) demands that the permanent siege, embargo, and cage-like existence end; that assassination of their leaders stop (Israel can pinpoint target persons by cell phone with drone laser technology): that they be labeled terrorists (by Israel and the United States); that they receive recognition of their own state (which they claim pre-dates Israel); and that settlements on their land be stopped and withdrawn.

Israel demands that rockets fired into Israel cease once and for all, that smuggling weapons be stopped along with terrorist bombings (e.g., in a Tel Aviv bus station this morning), and that her existence in Terra Sancta be acknowledged and honored. This demand is posited on the assumption that Palestine will ever remain a disarmed nation under Israeli supervision. All this is rooted in her disputed claim to have received the land from Golan to Sinai, from river to sea—from God's decree even if it were to demand eradication of the Palestinian people from that same land.

And so the impasse continues—now pushing out toward a century-long agony between a people who once were persecuted to near-extermination (by Christians—not Muslims) and another people that had nothing to do with this atrocity.

Back to 1 Timothy—I confess that when I seek to root my own vocation in the 1 Timothy passage, my greatest problem is this Karux matter. I have trouble getting my head and arms around herald, announcer, watchman on the wall, messenger. I'm also not sure what the message is. I know how dangerous it is to be an unclear trumpet and how frightening it is to have no one follow an uncertain sound. I'm not sure whether the message—kerygma—is salvation in life and the world or salvation from life and the world, or some subtle blending of these.

Then there is the matter of teacher, i.e., master of didascalia—the truth tradition, the delivered deposit of truth, the heritage of belief, faith and creed. What is the content and substance of this so very crucial truth? Paul is crystal clear, a clarion call in his letter: "there is One God and One Mediator—a man—Christ Jesus" (1 Tim 2: 5). This is a conundrum for monotheism and Trinitarian doctrine but resolute even in mystery.

Then there is the target recipient—all humanity, "to the nations;" the *ethne*, all tribes and peoples; the myriad and diverse peoples of the oikoumene; the one world, creation of the one God.

This is all-important to me. It is my root quest in life, the impulse behind everything I do. It prompts my yearning to preach the gospel—wherever and whenever I can. It's behind our attempt to form small classes and groups like this to which we belong. It is the very essence of my vocation as a reader, thinker, writer, and speaker. Let me give an examples from a sample of my work from *The Ministry of Vincent Van Gogh in Religion and Art* (Eugene, OR: Wipf and Stock, 2012).

I have been intrigued with the instantiation of theological insight, moral power, and activated ministry in particular individuals—indeed every person, family, and nation. I am trying now to discern the meaning, message, and messenger that we find in this remarkable minister—in the apostle's word—evangelist, teacher, and pastor. My skill as a teacher of the church is put to a strenuous test in such a project. How do we recognize ministry in the endeavors—not narrowly in word and sacrament, as defined in the Reformed understanding of ministry, but now in paint, brush and correspondence?

First, I have to dive way over my head into the waters where art historians and secular philosophers swim. These waters swirl with skepticism regarding the being and presence of God in the world, anti-clericalism, and heightened emphasis of man as captain of his own soul. Vincent, in this enlightenment perspective, is post-religious, secular, humanistic, and his work is a hymn to nature and human transcendence. My retort, and perhaps contribution, to an appraisal to who he is and what his life means is that he is a worthy minister, seeking and finding new faith in ancient *truth*. Just as Paul the apostle found "new Being in a new age" in *Christus praesens*, so Vincent—with Kierkegaard—found a post-impressionistic, post-modern ethos of authentic being recovering "the lilies of the field" in a post-ecclesial gaze on God in the world.

In the end, ministry in truth, which is in *logos* (meaning), is efficacious—it works. In Vincent's favorite biblical words, "Light has shined in the world . . . so that humanity sees *good works* and Creator *Father* is glorified" (Matt 5:16). The process is harvest gathering to allude to his works. In the power of the Christ Spirit, Vincent's good works edify us as we are saved from false religion, from inhumanity and disdain, and violence toward the weak and poor. We are edified as our common life is centered in regard and care for the "least of these." To his ministry to the world, in return we minister to him in thanksgiving to God. We assure him that his work is not in vain—that God works as Vincent works. God has worked in and through Vincent. He belongs now to eternity and to the ages. Ministry is always reciprocal, yielding more than we ask or think (Eph 3:20).

BLACK FRIDAY AND ISRAEL BREAKS THE CEASE-FIRE— NOVEMBER 23, 2012

The twenty-year-old Palestinian has been shot in the head and killed—apparently by a soldier who fires first and aims later. The first casualty of the cease-fire. In Cairo, President Morsi assumes greater powers to undergird his commitments to broker the cease-fire and subsequent peace (e.g., superseding the judiciary) with Israel and Palestine and the peoples' protest in Tahrir Square. Meanwhile, we shop 'til we drop on Black Friday, which began on Turkey Thursday and continues 'til cyber Monday.

Lectionary-wise, we come upon Last Sunday of Pentecost and then Advent—now there's a paradoxical juxtaposition. Liturgical red transmutes into purple.

Fourteen

Advent Scriptural Reflections

First Week of Advent, December 2–9, 2012.

Promise Keepers.

IN THE JEREMIAH 33 service, I placed emphasis in class on the "almond rod" (branch or sprout), Jer 33 cf, Jer 1, 2, 23. The sect of Branch Davidians, Van Gogh's pictures of almond trees in early blossom, or of an almond sprig in a glass of water with, I wonder, a book which, I imagine, might offer some exegesis of "the stump of Jesse." I think, for example, of how Vincent sends a message from the book on the table of his canvas—his father's Bible open to Isaiah 53 or the *La joie de vivre* of Zola near a glass of absinthe.

The meaning of this rod or branch of righteousness is simply that the arising presence of God coming into the world is expressed as liberation, justice, love, and peace, i.e., the manifestations of righteousness—the hungry are fed; the homeless are sheltered; the prisoners are set free; and the poor receive the good news of help. I then related this to the conflict in Gaza/Israel; Syria, etc. Events this week included Palestine being given provisional status as state—with the United States, Israel, and a few others of the hundreds of world nations voting no (as the United States does on most good treaties and UN mandates). Meanwhile, Damascus and Gaza lie in rubble, Jordan writhes in turmoil, and we all wish we could reenact shepherds and sages arriving in Bethlehem bringing "peace on earth" despite our preference for violence and belligerence.

Hope messengers:

My class on Malachi 2, 3, and 4—restated in Luke 1: 16, 17—focused on the explication of the foregoing righteousness symptomatic of God's return and presence, as children and parents "turn their hearts back on each other" and general justice (*dikaiosune*) returns to persons and thereby to families, congregations, cities, states, nations, and the world.

Mighty to Save:

Zephaniah restates the same Advent/prophetic message. It is a message of unrestrained joy and ecstasy. God has redeemed and liberated his people. In other words, our wandering violence, injustice, and apostasy were trumped by the everlasting mercy and deliverance of a suffering servant—God's very self in the guise of a child who was born, a son who was given—who is wonderful Counselor, mighty Father, Prince of Peace (Isaiah 9). Listen to the prophet's words:

> For my determination is to gather the nations, that I may assemble the kingdoms, to pour upon them mine indignation, even all my fierce anger: for all the earth shall be devoured with the fire of my jealousy.
> For then will I turn to the people a pure language, that they may all call upon the name of the Lord, to serve him with one consent.
> From beyond the rivers of Ethiopia my suppliants, even the daughter of my dispersed, shall bring mine offering.
> In that day shalt thou not be ashamed for all thy doings, wherein thou hast transgressed against me: for then I will take away out of the midst of thee them that rejoice in thy pride, and thou shalt no more be haughty because of my holy mountain.
> I will also leave in the midst of thee an afflicted and poor people, and they shall trust in the name of the Lord.
> The remnant of Israel shall not do iniquity, nor speak lies; neither shall a deceitful tongue be found in their mouth: for they shall feed and lie down, and none shall make them afraid.
> Sing, O daughter of Zion; shout, O Israel; be glad and rejoice with all the heart, O daughter of Jerusalem.
> The Lord hath taken away thy judgments, he hath cast out thine enemy: the king of Israel, even the Lord, is in the midst of thee: thou shalt not see evil any more.

In that day it shall be said to Jerusalem, Fear thou not: and to Zion, Let not thine hands be slack.

The Lord thy God in the midst of thee is mighty; he will save, he will rejoice over thee with joy; he will rest in his love, he will joy over thee with singing.

I will gather them that are sorrowful for the solemn assembly, who are of thee, to whom the reproach of it was a burden.

Behold, at that time I will undo all that afflict thee: and I will save her that halteth, and gather her that was driven out; and I will get them praise and fame in every land where they have been put to shame.

At that time will I bring you again, even in the time that I gather you: for I will make you a name and a praise among all people of the earth, when I turn back your captivity before your eyes, saith the Lord.

My Comment: A universal reckoning and redeeming is on the way. To say that God is "mighty to save," to use the blithe divine solicitude as we do in that praise song, we need to know that God is mighty in salvation and damnation. Futuristic in Judaism and realized in Islam, we Christians read this paradise as already here—yet and not yet. Just as God was, is, and will be, so his kingdom came, has come, and will come. We work for it fervently for we know it is coming and, like a burning flame, it cannot be quenched. We also need to squash, once and for all, the moral absurdities, even blasphemies of the Christian right, with those like Mike Huckabee, who says that shootings in Newtown, Connecticut, are judgments on us for dropping prayer in the schools. To get things straight, we must ask what the features in our Zephaniah text are:

- A pure language—so all know how and whom to call, v. 9
- Both gathered and scattered—to Africa and beyond, v. 10
- Righteoused—background forgiven—buried in new endeavors of divine gift and human task. A new meaning to a new word—"primaried,"to v. 13
- New heart, speech, deeds and fearlessness, to v.16
- Home at last, to end of passage

Hanukkah—December 7, 2012:

Children twirl the dreidel as the celebration of lights is reenacted 2,200 years after Judas Maccabaeus's feat of defying the oppressing Hellenistic Roman king who would exterminate the light of Yahweh's faith. The background today is vivid—Gaza, Cairo, Damascus, and Jerusalem.

May I tell this story of darkness and the ascension of the light starting with a passage from Tom Friedman in yesterday's *New York Times* (December 5, 2012, A25).

> Tel Aviv
>
> I went to synagogue on Saturday not far from the Syrian border in Antakya [Tevye's Anatevka?], Turkey. It's been on my mind ever since.
>
> Antakya is home to a tiny Jewish community, which still gathers for holidays at the little Sephardic synagogue. It is also famous for its mosaic of mosques and Orthodox, Catholic, Armenian, and Protestant churches. How could it be that I could go to synagogue in Turkey on Saturday while on Friday, just across the Orontes River in Syria, I had visited with Sunni Free Syrian Army rebels embroiled in a civil war in which Syrian Alawites and Sunnis are killing each other on the basis of their ID cards, Kurds are creating their own enclave, Christians are hiding and the Jews are long gone?
>
> What is this telling us? For me, it raises the question of whether there are just three governing options in the Middle East today: Iron Empires, Iron Fists or Iron Domes?

After tracing the (1) benign overlordship of the Ottoman Empire, (2) the hard tyranny of the pre-Arab spring monarchs—Egypt's Mubarak, Libya's Quadaffi, and now Syria's Assad—threatening to use nerve gas rocket heads on his own people and, (3) Israel's complacent aggression against the Palestinians lulled into the delusion of safety by America-provided anti-rocket shield, this nervous onlooker asks: where do we locate our defensive and offensive security—in chariots, God, or human political maneuvers?

Tom Friedman concurs with my politically loaded question. Truth and justice alone will secure peace for Israel and Palestine. Jockeying for and assuming on military power didn't work for Goliath nor will iron empires, fists, domes, or masks. If all peace is derivative of the God of peace, only justice rolling down like waters will secure the peace in a two state—mutual affirmation—kind of settlement.

De-Christianizing the Holy Land or cleansing Muslims from Israel or Jews from Egypt and Palestine will make for permanent strife not permanent concord. Tom Friedman's vision of churches alongside synagogues and mosques is the only foundation for lasting justice and permanent peace and has a better chance to reconcile the three great religious peoples than does cleansed religious apartheid zones. Tevye is now a "wealthy man"; let's get on with healing the land.

Fifteen

More Shootings in Evanston, Illinois

Saturday, December 15, 2012—Christ Temple Missionary Baptist Church, 1711 Simpson, Evanston, Illinois.

OUR SEASONED PROS IN church issues and community violence—Marc Dennis, senior pastor of Second Baptist Church and Father Bob Oldershaw, emeritus priest at St. Nicholas Church—met yesterday with the chief of police of the city of Evanston. When I entered the church at 11 AM for the gun day, the chief greeted me, as I represented the ministerium on this day. I told my men's group in the early morning that I was commissioned because I was such a big target as well as being the only pastor who lived down in the ghetto. He said that we had a good two-pronged approach going—spirit and power—pastors and police. In my mind, the cycle of revenge killings had to stop and the only things that have ever worked were one person committed to a gesture of peace, not further violence—e.g., no Ireland or something like a truth commission in Africa. Maybe together we could get a handle on this crisis in my neighborhood with some such effort. Our home was on the red line between black and white Evanston. Could I be a bridge—pontifex minimus?

In this diary entry, which also includes chapter 16 in this book, I, (1) review the experience of this profound day. A crisis occurred in Evanston this last week, which on Friday was echoed around the world, together with a devastating shooting in Newtown, Connecticut, at Sandy Hook Elementary School; (2) I will then report a chronicle of events and my conversation with the remarkable woman, Carolyn Murray, who had planned the "gun return" day in an attempt to halt the crescendo in the cycle of violence in our home town; and finally, (3) I will offer my theological reflections on a season of work which brings anguish yet rays of hope and even joy—the joys of redemptive suffering.

The history of the crisis is complex yet profoundly simple. We have blunders in public policy and careless relocation decisions. We have a long and frustrating history of failed counter-efforts against gang violence. We have relentless rage and revenge that no one seems able to step up and stop. We have ineffective public and private response.

Evanston gangs have roots in Chicago gang history going back 100 years. From the original white to the European black leather gangs around Hyde Park, nothing has ever worked to prevent or intervent a destructive process. Today, with the profuse availability of weapons, the practice of killing goes on unabated. When public housing was torn down and families were resettled around the metropolitan area, gang ties moved with residents to new places like Evanston. As in the Americo-European decision to implant Israel in 1948 in Palestine, no careful planning was undertaken to facilitate the implantation of new people into an old community. As in the case of Chicago, a one-hundred-year span of conflicted history is the cost nations of the world are paying for the European holocaust or the injustices in immigrant America.

KAIROS OR KRISIS

Transpiring moments such as now require careful contemplation, preparation, and follow-through. They require an individual and corporal construal—issues are immediate and structural. My involvement with the present upheaval in Evanston began with the Dajae Coleman—Wes Woodson case (see late September/early October entries in this memoir. My neighbor, twenty-year-old Wes Woodson III—killed Dajae in a fit of animosity ending in a haphazard shooting one night when he had been told that one of his "family members" had been knifed down Church Street at the high school. He heard that the guy with the weapon was from a competing family gang. It turns out that this case is actually isolated from the broader cluster of cases that ensued down west on the same blocks (1700) of Brown and Gray streets and alleys. After the Dajae case, I was away for a few weeks to do some political seminars in Ohio and Wisconsin. I had just recently returned to my home at the sixteen hundred block of Ashland (Woodson is at 1706), to find the community reeling from this rash of murders. Here is the saga of what has been going on (the draft is rough and subject to revision).

Chronology

- Justin Bamberg (23) was killed at 1700 Gray—Tuesday, early AM—December 11 2012.
- His brother, Javar Bamberg (22), was killed shortly thereafter in the alley of 1700 Gray Ave.
- Justin Murray of 1800 Brown Ave, nineteen-year-old son of Carolyn Murray, was killed a week ago in front of his grandmother's house down the street.
- Carolyn Murray (divorced from James Copeland) is aunt to the Bamberg boys and Robert Gresham.
- Robert Gresham (22), half brother to John and Javar Bramberg, was killed on June 19, 2005, at "The Keg" (local pub) by Antoine Hill, who then spent five years in prison before he was released from prison September 24, 2010.
- On September 30, 2010, Marcus Davis was killed as he backed out of Smitty's Auto Shop on Dodge Street (near Evanston Township High School). He was killed by John Bamberg (26).
- Bamberg was found not guilty of the murder of Marcus Davis.
- On December 8, 2012, a yet unidentified twenty-year-old was shot at 1900 Howard Street. His name came up in the Murray examination. He is now on life support at St. Francis Hospital in Evanston.

Sixteen

Obama in Newtown

The President's Pastoral—Newtown, Connecticut, December 16, 2012.

ONLY LITURGY CAN RESPOND to such a Litany and Lament.
"We've endured too many of these tragedies in the past few years, and each time I learn the news, I react not as a President, but as anyone else would—as a parent. And that was especially true today," Obama said. "I know there's not a parent in America who does not feel the same overwhelming grief as I do."

"Our hearts are broken today," Obama added.

Noting other recent shootings, including the massacre at an Aurora, Colorado, movie theater in July, Obama added, "As a country, we have been through this too many times."

Obama also emphasized the need to take action against the rash of shootings, "regardless of the politics," in an apparent reference to the debate over gun control in America.

The President ended his speech with a Scripture quote, intoning, "May God bless the memory of the victims and, in the words of Scripture, heal the broken-hearted and bind up their wounds."

"By any standards of human and moral decency, children in America are under assault, and by international standards, America remains an unparalleled world leader in gun deaths of children and teens—a distinction we shamefully and immorally choose! The most recent analysis of data from 23 high-income countries reported that 87 percent of children under age 15 killed by guns in these nations lived in the United States. And the U.S. gun homicide rate for teens and young adults 15 to 24 was 42.7 times higher than the combined gun homicide rate for that same age group in the other countries" ("Protect Children Not Guns 2012," p. 7, Children's Defense Fund, www.childrensdefense.org).

At the evening Prayer Service at the memoriam at Sandy Hook School, Newtown, Connecticut, on December 16, 2012 President Obama said, in part:

> This is our first task, caring for our children. It's our first job. If we don't get that right, we don't get anything right. That's how, as a society, we will be judged.
>
> And by that measure, can we truly say, as a nation, that we're meeting our obligations?
>
> Can we honestly say that we're doing enough to keep our children, all of them, safe from harm?
>
> Can we claim, as a nation, that we're all together there, letting them know they are loved and teaching them to love in return?
>
> Can we say that we're truly doing enough to give all the children of this country the chance they deserve to live out their lives in happiness and with purpose?
>
> I've been reflecting on this the last few days, and if we're honest with ourselves, the answer's no. We're not doing enough. And we will have to change.
>
> We will be told that the causes of such violence are complex, and that is true. No single law, no set of laws can eliminate evil from the world or prevent every senseless act of violence in our society, but that can't be an excuse for inaction. Surely we can do better than this.
>
> Are we really prepared to say that we're powerless in the face of such carnage, that the politics are too hard?
>
> Are we prepared to say that such violence visited on our children year after year after year is somehow the price of our freedom?
>
> You know, all the world's religions, so many of them represented here today, start with a simple question.
>
> Why are we here? What gives our life meaning? What gives our acts purpose?
>
> There's only one thing we can be sure of, and that is the love that we have for our children, for our families, for each other.
>
> "Let the little children come to me," Jesus said, "and do not hinder them, for to such belongs the kingdom of heaven."

Familially and in community, we must get back to the Torah ways of justice, mercy, and peace—before it is too late.

INTERVIEW WITH CAROLYN MURRAY

Carolyn Murray is a lovely young professional woman with a keen sense of religious faith and civic responsibility. A military leader, she has lived abroad and has a wide appreciation of various faiths and of the interconnection of vibrant faith and vital ethics. Her sponsorship of the gun return exemplifies this worldview and she has a fine-tuned sense of theodicy (why does this happen since God is good?) and an acute pastoral practice. She lives in my neighborhood and has been directly affected by this extraordinary spate of recent killings. We in Evanston know acutely the profound grief of Newtown, for we have been hit just as hard. We hear Rachel crying for her children who are no more, and Carolyn especially bears this pain in her heart, having lost her own child and several nephews.

With Pastor Cherry's introduction, I asked Carolyn to sit down as I posed a few questions. Thirty feet in front of us in the church hall were two dozen armed and protective-geared police as they ingathered some one hundred weapons. I first asked her what gave her the idea for the gun turn in. The idea had been brewing for many days. Before Justin was killed, she frequently had visitors on her front porch—at the ominous hours of one or four am, affirming her gun conviction, and then shooting off their guns. When she summoned the police—who are always only seconds away—no one was there.

The mirage or actual visitation strengthened her resolve on the gun plan. Someone, she said, had to stop the vicious cycle of revenge. I told her of my own experience, even as a skeptical professor type, of being prompted by the presence of Dajae to get on with my political work in Ohio—that he was okay. I went on to ask her why this all was happening now and for so many years. Tears flooded her eyes as she spoke of her own faults raising adolescents. She spoke of Justin's faults and weaknesses. She spoke of the tensions, the neglect, and even the hatred of the white community in Evanston, Chicago, and the nation against blacks. The young people had no jobs, no mentors, no hope. As the only white guy in the ministry team there that day, we agreed that the community pastors should get their act together. Then and only then could we sing in solidarity... "black and white together... We shall overcome."

My Commentary: The ancient Moloch—the child-incinerating god and his death pit (Gehenna) south of Jerusalem is alive and well today. We sacrifice our children daily—en masse. We profuse their video and audio culture daily with violence, and we fill the world with violence, exporting most of the guns, ammunitions, and land mines. We kill our children as we allow, condone, and even desire violence. We do not object to violence, assuming in some perverted theology that we will always have the poor and the victims before us, or offering blasphemies and sacrileges such as was heard from one southern pastor-politico—"the killing in Newtown was because we stopped prayer in the school."

We sacrifice our children daily to the harmful gods of business, negligence, indulgence and, in general, we expect of youth accountability and responsibility, all the while offering them strong support, mentoring, and tutelage. We abandon them too readily in laissez-faire aloneness to joblessness, poor education, and, beyond depression, the despair of "no way out."

Adolescents (fifteen to twenty-five) are not given—as they are in most cultures in the world—responsibility for meal preparation, guest entertainment, home maintenance, real hard study, Sabbath worship, and learning—as well as leadership. They should be encouraged insistently in their gifts—music, arts, languages, craftsmanship. We should not accept the cop-out, opt-out excuse that they are not smart (they are), that they are sick e.g., autism and Asperger's syndrome, (they are very gifted), and we should not promulgate the Marine invitation: "we need a few good men—but sorry—we already have too many."

My overriding reflection in times such as these is that we need—one and all—to enter into deep repentance: "I have sinned, I have done and left undone—I have unclean hands and lips and I dwell amid a people of unclean lips." We must also heed those mighty words, "whoever causes one of these little ones to stumble—it would be better . . ." Let us individually, and societally, repent and bring forth the fruits worthy of repentance.

December 22, 2012: Funeral of Javar Bamberg.

A gentle chill falls on Evanston this Christmastide. Everyone has eased into travels or receiving family home for the holidays. It is a time of unease. Fiscal crisis looms as a newly reelected President Obama struggles with a totally intransigent right wing majority in the House of Representatives. Syria descends into terminal chaos and the butchering of her citizens. One of the world's great civilizations has been ruined, set back a thousand years—another victim of Franco-Anglo-American colonial manipulations and American/Israeli-Arab/Islamic contortions that have so despoiled the fates of ancient tribes in our modern world. Beneath the surface agonies lies, I regret, a lethal animosity between Jews and Christians (especially Islamophobic evangelicals) on the one hand and Muslims on the other. Interfaith persons like myself seem to be a disappearing minority.

A mad imperial tyrant has turned murderer on his own people and the poor continue to be exploited here at home. In Evanston, Chicago, and the United States, our disgraceful violence at the top has turned us against our own flesh and blood, as outrage shootings of children at the grassroots of our culture reflect the violent demagoguery at the very apex of American belligerence and materialism in the world. Tomorrow is Christmas Sunday and our gift box is marked "Fragile: Handle with Care"—instructions we are very unlikely to heed. As our children celebrate the lights and sing the songs we fear for their futures.

A slight frost covers the momentarily tranquil town while everyone wonders when the next shoe will drop. In Evanston, multiple young lives have been snuffed out, aided by our ubiquitous weaponry—even as the NRA's sinister policies assure that guns—even war weapons— are readily available, cruising without jeopardy across state and national lines by this nation that manufactures and markets most of the guns, bombs, and land mines in the world. Meanwhile, we show what we believe and value by what we reject: treaties to protect the environment, to care for handicapped persons, to restrict weapons of killing. America has within its borders 5 percent of the world's citizens and 50 percent of its guns. Eighty-seven percent of the world's gun killings in the past year occurred in our nation, and we all fear for our children, our neighbors, and ourselves.

So, today another funeral is about to begin. The Bamberg family is part of an extended network of families in Evanston that has experienced ten or more gang killings in recent years. Our Evanston ministerium, as I have earlier noted in this memoir, decided to amalgamate the black and white minister's association after the Dajae Coleman killing. The ministerium has now assumed a vocation of reconciliation among the communities if we can only stop the cycle of revenge killings and deal with the special problem of sanctuary and hiding for those threatened with further killings. Minister Ishmael Muhammad delivers the eulogy for Javar Bamberg, as he had for Justin Murray. His message is thoroughly biblical, Christological, and truthful. The bullet-proof-vested Evanston Police Department stand by and ready.

Concluding the year can best be expressed by two passages from hymns of the season, followed by a sermon on the eve before New Year's Eve given at the historic Lincoln family church where I used to serve and continue to watch over as I do in my home city and church in Evanston. David's royal city contains a hauntingly relevant petition to God as we seek to limp through the end of a year in "such a time as this." The same for a passage from Martin Luther's Christmas hymn, "On Christian Freedom," published in the year 1520 (from *Luther's Works*, Fortress Press):

> "And He leads his children on, to the place where He has gone..."
> "Bless all the dear children in thy tender care, and take them to heaven to live with thee there..."

Seventeen

Homily, Second Presbyterian Church—Getting Bolder, Bigger, and Better

First Sunday after Christmas Day.

Sermon preached at Second Presbyterian Church, Chicago, December 30, 2012.

Text: "Your sons and daughters will prophesy, your old men will dream dreams and your young men shall see visions and whoever calls on the Name of the Lord will be delivered" (Joel 2: 28 and Acts 2:17).

SERMON NOTES

THE CALL TO BE a prophet came to Jeremiah in the year 625 BCE during the reigns of the last Kings of Judah. It was an acute moment of promise—the promised and promising kingdom of King David was at hand. We pick up the narrative with Abraham Heschel's classic translation of Jeremiah in his book—*The Prophets* (New York: Harper Perennial, 2001):

> The Word of the Lord came to me saying, Before I formed you in the womb I knew you, and before you were born I consecrated you. I appointed you a prophet to the nations. Then I said, ah, Lord God, behold I do not know how to speak for I am only a youth. But the Lord said to me, do not say I am only a youth; for to all to whom I send you, you shall go, and whatever I command you, you shall speak, be not afraid of them for I am with you to deliver you, says the Lord. Then the Lord touched my mouth, and the Lord said to me. Behold I have put my words on your mouth, see I have

set you this day over nations and over kingdoms, to pluck up and to break down, to destroy and overthrow, to build and plant.

The kingdom Jeremiah is sent to announce and enact is the kingdom of David. What was this strange thing—a kingdom? Young Bar and Bat Mizvahs of that time—like our catechumens today—had a vague idea; people still talked about one named David, a scrawny teenager who led his frightened family and friends against a Goliath with his impenetrable armor and indefensible shield and spear. But what was David's kingdom now when Judea was weak and helpless against powerful armies like those of America and Israel today? The giant from Gath—Gaza and Philistia—Palestine today, in that day had the slingshot as they do today. Was the kingdom of David a Camelot, a happy-ever-after land somewhere way back, or was it a state of affairs in some dreamed for future?

In seeking answers to those questions we are back to Jeremiah's vision. He says again, "And the word of the Lord came to me again, saying—Jeremiah, what do you see, and I said "I see a rod—a branch of almond." Then the Lord said to me, "You have seen well, for *I am watching over you to perform it*" (Jer 1: 11–12). Now this whole thing is getting pretty crazy! Hard to understand, elusive, incomprehensible, something like this confusing time today. I had the great honor of being with Abraham Joshua Heschel the last night of his life in the 1970s when we protested the arrest of Father Phil Berrigan, SJ, at the Groton navy base in Connecticut. He had just chained himself to a nuclear ship.

Heschel felt that he had seen the beginning of the coming, at last, of that promised kingdom—when in 1967 the impediments to the partitioning wall dividing David's palace and monarch citadel—Jerusalem—fell, and he could, at last, offer his laments and hopes at the wailing wall. Jews had offered this oblation from the time of Herod—builder of the Second Temple, Eli, Elkanah, their son, John the Baptist, Jesus, James, Jesus' brother, and all the rest who have bent the back and cried the tears at the "wailing wall." Yet today, at Christmas 2012, that wall is still drenched with the tears of the Messiah-Emmanuel and the human race which is his people.

Like Jesus, Heschel would today weep over the city—knowing a peace that eluded that Jeru' salam—that intended place of peace on earth established in justice. He would grieve with the tears of Joshua (Jesus) and Jeremiah seeing what is going on at the justice frontier today and the terrible complicity of church, synagogue, and nations in our perverse and profuse anti-justice and anti-peace, moving from metaphor to meaning Christians come down at this axis of the history of God to establish their faith. Jews yearn for a kingdom brought in by a Davidic servant—one yet to come one—or more often a whole people who would end the scourge of history and make peace in Terra Sancta. Today, this state of affairs seems more remote than ever. Muslims speak of an almond tree that will become a tree of life for all people. Allah of Semitic conviction, el'lah of Jesus, and El Eschad—the one God of Israel—will one day, perhaps soon, in an imminent time horizon, form a reconciled and redeemed world people, a global kingdom of Messiah, Lord, Christos, a called community, an Ummah.

An originally good creation—one then despoiled and contorted by human violence and forgetfulness—is now made whole, and well by God's Spirit. This is this realm that at last will arise on the earth. The Bible is very complicated and confusing on this point. *Kingdom* seems to be here, there, and both here and there. It is now, then, and both now and then. So much for Scripture's rendition of what Einstein calls time and space and his followers call the "theory of everything." In crude anthropomorphism we call this the kingdom of David or the kingdom of God. Youth should try to enlist as "child soldier."

Out of this crucible of crisis—a virtual Herodian infanticide—a faint call comes and is reluctantly heard: "Go now my young friends and tell my message to the nations of the world." And like Samuel and Jeremiah, we still, rather than trying to refresh old saws or find new clichés or shibboleths ask, "Who am I—what can I say?" "Am I a child soldier; do I have a bullet-proof vest?" I will give you what to say, answers the Lord in his word. We hear Isaiah 61—the day will come—if only you do my will—when we will "no longer raise our children for destruction and all persons will grow into maturity and enjoy long years."

With this foundation established, let us in conclusion look at two concrete proposals on how we can advocate and activate a youth ministry that is true to Scripture and tradition. This is the only way that society can be healed. The last verse in the Old Testament and the first in the New gets at this truth—the messianic days—the day of the Lord will come even as evil is amplified and ominous clouds cling all around. It will get so bad, all Scriptures say, that parents will betray their children and children their parents. "I will turn the hearts of the parents to the children and the hearts of the children to the parents—lest I come and smite the earth with a curse" (Mal 4:6, Luke 1:17).

Youth can only take up their rightful ministry as child soldiers for the prince of peace if they lay hold of that ministry for themselves. Our adult world must demand and undergird that "child soldiers"—faithful and true to the one living God of Scripture and creation. It is time for children to become little Samuel in the ephod made by mom or Jesus in the Jerusalem Temple in the one made by his mom. It is time for Sam and Josh—Samantha and Jess. It is the moment for each one of you here today to don the linen ephod or the Jesus street tunic with tassel phylacteries (Scripture capsules)—and "increase in wisdom, stature and favor with God and people" (Luke 2:52).

Today 30 percent of Americans, 50 percent of residents of cities, wish to be known as "nones." They write down "none of the above when asked to identify their faith." Sometimes they play the old game: "I'm spiritual but not religious." I can worship "my God" on the golf course, in Bloomingdales or Starbucks. They have no time for that old oxymoron: "organized religion." Again Josh (Jesus) leads the way: "I must be about my "father's business;" my base of operations is my "father's house." Here is where judgment begins—in church. This is why the president is *Time* magazine's Person of the Year, and we hope God's person of the year, and has called on people of faith to get us back on the God course. My friends, the times are too urgent to be "none of the above." Sara and I have been reading Lucretius's *On the Nature of Things* this holiday. We ask you to join us in a commitment to be more religious humanists and humanist religionists—the world needs such now as never before.

Sunday, December 30, 2012.

Year C, Revised Common Lectionary.

> 1 Samuel 2:18–20, 26: Samuel was ministering before the Lord, a boy wearing a linen ephod. His mother used to make for him a little robe and take it to him each year, when she went up with her husband to offer the yearly sacrifice. Then Eli would bless Elkanah and his wife, and say, "May the Lord repay you with children by this woman for the gift that she made to theLord"; and then they would return to their home. Now the boy Samuel continued to grow both in stature and in favor with the Lord and with the people.

Luke 2:41–52: Now every year his parents went to Jerusalem for the festival of the Passover. And when he was twelve years old, they went up as usual for the festival. When the festival was ended and they started to return, the boy Jesus stayed behind in Jerusalem, but his parents did not know it. Assuming that he was in the group of travelers, they went a day's journey. Then they started to look for him among their relatives and friends. When they did not find him, they returned to Jerusalem to search for him. After three days they found him in the temple, sitting among the teachers, listening to them and asking them questions. And all who heard him were amazed at his understanding and his answers. When his parents saw him they were astonished; and his mother said to him, "Child, why have you treated us like this? Look, your father and I have been searching for you in great anxiety." He said to them, "Why were you searching for me? Did you not know that I must be in my Father's house?" But they did not understand what he said to them. Then he went down with them and came to Nazareth, and was obedient to them. His mother treasured all these things in her heart. And Jesus increased in wisdom and in years, and in divine and human favor.

SERMON: GETTING BOLDER, BIGGER, AND BETTER

"He increased in wisdom, stature and in favor of God and man."

The six year old first grader could not wait to meet the president. He had helped escort his classmates out of Sandy Hook Elementary School in Newtown, Connecticut. The president leaned down to hear the lad's story. "Don't worry, Mr. President—I'll lead my friends out—I can do karate." Something like the boldness of the twelve-year-old in our text who felt at home with the scholars in the temple—though his weapon was slightly different—kerygma (News), not karate.

The Samuel/Jesus compound is a fascinating Scripture as we ponder the ministry of young people today and the particular challenges they face in this world which seems so out of sorts, especially when measured against this season of peace on earth and good will toward people.

A little child—Samuel by name—dons his tiny homemade robe as his priest father and mother carry out the sacrificial prayers in the temple. Jesus is also a youth as he tarries in the temple—in interrogation and debate—quite to the consternation of his parents. The summary snapshot of Samuel then appropriated to Jesus will cover long years of development with these few words: "He increased in wisdom, stature and in favor of God and people."

The next we hear of Jesus is his abrupt appearance out of Galilee into the Jordan Valley where he asks for baptism from that birth-contemporary—John the Baptist. The liturgy is already ominous as the words from the Bethlehem angels now become the words about Abraham's sacrifice of Isaac—"this is my son—the only and beloved child." These words imply that he who was born in the stable was the One who would be lifted up. In an important third entanglement, his mother Mary, who pondered this projected meaning and destiny for her child, is woven into the Samuel narrative as the gospel writers borrow Hannah's song in Luke 1 for Mary's Magnificat: "He shall take down the mighty from their seats and lifted up those of low degree."

Today we welcome peace on earth, and all around us children are being killed as in those days of King Herod. Mystery shrouds the whole thing, of course, since we cannot see or comprehend God, for God's thoughts and ways are not ours. At first, as we celebrate in this season, it is Magnum Mysterium; only the animals—the ox and the ass, the sheep and donkey—only the beasts can see. Even *Family Guy* gets it wrong in his journey of the holy family to Bethlehem. The obstetrician cannot be called out to deliver at night, and he doesn't make house calls. So the animals huddle around and consult—"what shall we name him?" asks the donkey all shaggy and brown. "It's a no brainer," says the cow, all white and red. And the all-wise cow says, "he was born in the barn; we'll call him Barney." So much for bovine wisdom.

The peace on earth and good will delivered by the manger child-king is called the kingdom of David. What does that mean? David and his branch, his seed, his rod is spoken of as an almond branch. In Israel and Islam (our primary and secondary corroborations of Christian Scripture) the almond branch is called the *tisch bisvot*, the healing gathering of trees—what Handel also lyricized as "trees where you sit, coming into a shade"—now each in the scorching sun can sit under his own fig tree. This is also a "tree of life" as seen in a paradise garden or in the door of the mosque. It is a hardy, glorious branch as painter Vincent Van Gogh depicted—a scrawny, unappealing scrub that blossoms into a splendorous mustard-yellow bush. This is the root out of dry ground of which Isaiah 53 speaks. This is the child king that Isaiah 9 speaks of—he shall be

Homily, Second Presbyterian Church   171

called wonderful counselor, mighty God, everlasting Father, and prince of peace, and his kingdom will have no end. Handel thought that this spoke of the Christian Messiah. That child king, that child soldier, is a new kind of warrior. One who is born in the city of David—Christ the Lord.

In light of this understanding, today in Bethlehem, Newtown, Damascus, and Chicago, the hearts of all the children of Abraham and their almond branches throughout the earth yearn for this coming and pray in Aramaic/Arabic: *maranatha*, "come quickly," as if we could abide it if it were to come. Handel calls here on another youth prophet—"who shall stand when he appeareth?" Inference—no one! No, not one, for all have sinned and fallen short and that servant who comes, "He is like a refiners fire," and he shall purify the sons of Levi and offer, at last, at long last, when all is ready, an offering of righteousness—and creation will be set right. But first things must be set right and this entails justice, which has to begin in the house of God. Repentance and righteousness begin here.

This biblical and contemporary material is on our heart and mind today on this youth Sunday. Also on my heart and yours perhaps are six other teenage boys whose mothers in Evanston cry out like Rachel for lost sons who are no more, and six others—the mothers of those youth who shot and killed their own neighbors—these moms also lost sons these recent weeks, sons who will spend most of the rest of their lives in prison. Our heart also aches for the little ones mowed down in Newtown, Connecticut. Their little bodies were violated with gangland machine gun executions, as in Al Capone's Cicero or by Nazi rifle practice, depicted in *Shindler's List*. Rachel's cry now grips America and the whole world—and heaven weeps with us—"when will you ever learn?"

And so it is in the city of David today—a garrisoned, walled, apartheid city. Nearby Gaza lies in shambles and just to the east lies Damascus, where a young Hillel rabbi named Saul was called to bring a message to the nations, the Gentiles, and an imagined Abrahamic ruler—an opthamologist, (apparently blind) named Assad—rains Russian scud missiles and cluster bombs on his own people, even in bread lines where the famed synagogue and the Alleppo Codex are. And the cacophonous—Bosch—scream and wail arises now from our little town of Bethlehem (Newtown) and resonates across the shepherd's fields of Columbine, Aurora, Phoenix, Evanston, and Chicago. In desperation we cry out "where next?" and we carry out the bodies of our children.

The Bible speaks in a strange and sublime logic. It simply says, "don't believe this—but this"—"Don't do this, but this." No other gods—only this God. Do not kill—enrich life—and so on. In expositing our text of today, this means don't stupefy, stunt, and sicken my children whom I have entrusted into your care. Rather, help them increase in wisdom, stature, and favor—with God, and people. Great forces continually arise in this world against this truth and way.Ignorance, want, sickness, death, violence, and failure to thrive. But good news has come, and we go tell it on the mountain. The Bethlehem visitor who is Emmanuel assures us—"The One who is in you is stronger than he who is in the world" (1 John 4: 4).

One beautiful benediction is that Mr. Rogers is back in the news. Fred Rogers, we remember, is a Presbyterian pastor. Even better, he is an adult-child or child-adult—an uncanny, arresting, put on the lab-coat, get on the floor, kind of person. He is a child soldier in his cardigan or play jacket. This week, his counsel to the society at the time of the killing of Robert F. Kennedy was recalled. "I plead for your protection and support of our children," he said in his gentle, accepting manner. Mr. Rogers asked that we love our children and all of the world's children and not submit them further to violence and hatred—so they might grow up to be well and strong. This is the will and wish of the giver and receiver of life. The words became viral, along with the photo of Mr. Rogers kneeling down to the little lad at a Pittsburgh hospital who wished to touch his face.

If you have an evening for a film this Epiphany, catch *Les Miserables*, after the book and play by Victor Hugo. Jean Valjean is the Christ figure, helping and healing the poor little ones of his Paris world against a Javert regime of violence. Sing along as it proclaims its watchword (and ours), "Bring Him Home." "To love another person is to see the face of God."

May we, in this nativity season, see the rebirth of goodness on Earth as we see the face of God in the eyes of that tender babe who, in Dickens indelible metaphor, has gathered all the children of the earth stunted by ignorance and want under the cloak of the Ghost of Christmas Present, and let us declare a new year of recommitment. So with Tennyson, let us ring out the old, ring in the new, ring out the false, ring in the true, ring out old shapes of foul disease, ring out the narrowing lust for gold, ring out the thousand years of war, ring in the thousand years of peace (Alfred Lord Tennyson, 1850, "Ring Out Wild Bells," from *In Memoriam*,—an elegy to his sister's betrothed, who died at the age of twenty-two). In the name of Father, Son, and Spirit, and his people say—Amen!

Eighteen

Excursus: Last Days of 2012

Is it a beginning or an ending? Do we approach a cliff with a collapse of all our savings and retirement provisions—including Medicare—or will the improving economy be allowed to proceed? Perhaps our better instincts (and angels) will prevail or perhaps Grover (Norquist) will win the day as he promises to "reduce the nation's government to the size of a bathtub and drown it." Here in Evanston, hope springs eternal with the holidays and the fresh cover of snow—shielding our bloody sins all over the ground, "though they be as scarlet" (Ps 51:7). Even here God washes clean, refreshes, and renews.

But the news is sobering, calling us to enter the new year with repentance and resolve. We have surpassed five hundred gun killings in Chicago this past year. That does not include our lot in Evanston. This is a far greater sum than Los Angeles or New York City, and these cities have larger populations. Jesse Jackson—with his other agonies over children—finds the cause in guns and drugs arriving in droves. We know the manufacturers and sellers—and jobs departing. Most of the carnage is that prophesied by his fellow minister at Javar Bamberg's funeral: black-on-black children killing their own flesh and blood. "If the top of the society is wayward, what should we expect at the bottom?"

www.ingramcontent.com/pod-product-compliance
Lightning Source LLC
Chambersburg PA
CBHW050809160426
43192CB00010B/1699